RICHARD PETTY

IMAGES OF THE KING

BEN BLAKE AND DICK CONWAY

MOTORBOOKS

First published in 2005 by Motorbooks, an imprint of MBI Publishing Company, Galtier Plaza, Suite 200, 380 Jackson Street, St. Paul, MN 55101-3885 USA

Motorbooks titles are also available at discounts in bulk quantity for industrial or sales-promotional use. For details write to Special Sales Manager at Motorbooks Wholesalers & Distributors, Galtier Plaza, Suite 200, 380 Jackson Street, St. Paul, MN 55101-3885 USA.

ISBN 0-7603-2041-1

Editors: Lee Klancher and Leah Noel
Designer: Mandy Iverson

Printed in China

On the cover: Now, more than 10 years since he stopped driving, Richard Petty is known as much for his iconic look—feathered cowboy hat and sunglasses—as for his unbelievable racing career. *Dick Conway*

On the endpapers: A typical racing toolbox, circa 1976. *Dick Conway*

On the frontispiece: Petty was the first NASCAR driver to build strong sponsor identification. He became STP's flag carrier in 1972, and many racing fans don't remember a time that the No. 43 car wasn't STP red and blue. *Dick Conway*

On the title page: "The King" looks to the road ahead while Dale Inman leans in to talk about the impending race. *Dick Conway*

On the back cover: "The King" at ease while timing laps from the comfort of the garage. *Dick Conway*

CONTENTS

RICHARD IS WHAT HE IS: "THE KING"

═

"What makes winners and losers?
I don't know . . . .
Maybe my personality,
my ability, and all that,
happened to come at a time
when the sport could use it."

R ichard Petty operates on his own clock. I learned this firsthand when I made a visit to Petty Enterprises in 1992, ready to sit down with "The King" for an hour to talk about his impending retirement from racing.

Well, *two* hours into this interview, just as the greatest figure to emerge from American motorsports was getting warmed up, his longtime scheduler and family friend Martha Jane Bonkemeyer poked her head in to let him know he had just a few more things on his schedule that day.

Everyone who has known Richard Petty for a while knows Martha Jane has done this many times over the years—not because "The King" is irresponsible or unmindful. It's more that Richard Petty—in his steadfast certainty that he is no better or no worse than any farmer, machinist, or king of Sweden—has always treated everyone equally, or even better than that. His philosophy spells out like this: If *you're* here, everyone else can wait a minute. This is part of the reason he became such an American icon, the man who made NASCAR a household word and secured its long-term success.

The next time I visited Level Cross, which then was nothing more than a rural cross-roads off U.S. 220 in North Carolina, I was there to visit the new Petty Museum. The museum, now in a new building in Randleman, welcomes at least 25,000 visitors a year. It is well-designed and simple, and you can't help but wonder how much memorabilia had to be left out of the original 5,000-some-square-foot space.

The museum's highlights include a dead-on replica of the 1959 Oldsmobile Lee Petty drove to victory in the inaugural Daytona 500. Just across from it is the "blaze of glory" Pontiac Richard drove in his last race at Atlanta in 1992, the paint still blistered along the

NASCAR's early evolution was often spurred by what the Pettys championed. Richard, in the 1960s, helped pioneer use of the window nets, which were designed to keep the driver's head safely inside the cage in case of a violent wreck. *Dick Conway*

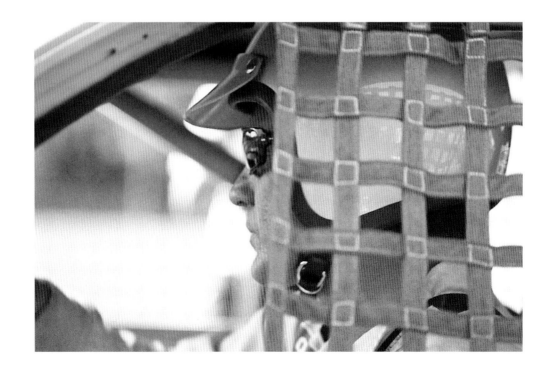

bottom panels from the engine fire that sidelined him. Toward the front sits a tableau of a 1950 Plymouth coupe, unrestored, with a crate of Mason jars suggesting NASCAR racing's moonshine origins. That's a touch perhaps added by the curators or consultants who helped create the museum. I've never heard much that would mix Lee Petty, or any of the Pettys, with the illegal liquor trade.

What's most impressive about the Petty Museum is a row of glass cases and wall displays that runs down the center of the exhibit space. In these areas, the Petty family has vouchsafed mementos and documentation of the many honors Richard Petty has received from all kinds of people—police chiefs, fire departments, governors, Little League teams, presidents of the United States, charitable societies, NFL teams—there are even White House dinner place cards showing that Richard and Lynda sat with the prime minister of Israel and other world figures.

You walk down that row and realize that each one, each and every one, of those items of honoraria indicates a ceremony, a heartfelt honor, with Richard (as always) smiling and holding a particular plaque as photographers flashed away. Literally thousands of these captured moments are lined up here. Then you head to the next row over—a collection of gold- and silver-plate beauties from as far back as the 1950s, some tarnished, all jewels. Some come from tracks long forgotten—giant, ornate concoctions from Columbia, South Carolina, or Oma, West Virginia. There's also the NASCAR owner trophy from Richard's first championship in 1964, presented to Lee Petty, the car's listed owner.

Dozens and dozens and dozens of accolades fill this space, all basically acknowledging this sentiment: OK guys, here's what we've done, more or less.

Richard takes time out to talk with members of the Drewry Mason High School marching band at Martinsville in 1975. The local high school band had the honor of performing before races at the homey Virginia oval.
Dick Conway

All of this showcases what you already know—Richard Petty is a figure larger than ordinary and at the same time strangely ordinary. He has spent 40-plus years working out the balance between two sides of himself, a regular guy and an extraordinary talent who maximized his abilities in a unique time and place. He is a man who sat and talked with presidents and kings, yet anyone on earth can walk up to him and strike up a conversation. And no matter who they are, Richard Petty won't act much differently than he would during a White House visit. That is one of Richard Petty's special skills—one at the heart of his nature; it never seems forced or difficult.

Part of what made Petty, and ultimately NASCAR, a growing success in the 1970s was that "The King," the most popular and winningest of drivers, never shied away from spending time with his fans. Here fans pass programs over a fence so Petty can sign them. *Dick Conway*

The other, and most prominent, of his special skills was driving a race car. From 1958, when he was just a strapping, sun-tanned youth, to 1992, when he walked away from the steering wheel for the last, heartbreaking time, he set records so monumental that they will never be equaled. I can say that for a fact. No one will ever start 1,184 NASCAR races and win 200 of them again; no one will win 27 of those races in one year, including 10 in a row. These achievements are singular. Don't bother trying to top them.

But Petty, even long into retirement, puts these matters into context: They're unbelievable in a way, but they come down to being the right man, in the right place, at the right time. "The only credit I can take is I was just here when it happened," he says.

"What makes winners and losers? I don't know. Nobody can tell me. Reflexes and eyesight, I mean, these cats probably are all compatible on that stuff. Nobody's got any better reflexes or much better eyesight, know what I mean? They just put it together better, and what does that, I don't know.

"Maybe my personality, my ability, and all that, happened to come at a time when the sport could use it. And it's going to be a long time before anybody comes into racing who can take it and ride with it in the expansion it had when I was there."

How true. Stars come and stars go, but no one carried NASCAR on his back for 30-plus years—willing and cheerfully—the way Richard Petty did. Jeff Gordon may be the closest modern analog, but he isn't even close. Just think of what A. J. Foyt would say: Check the record book.

Some years later, I visited the Petty property again, this time while working on this book. The physical plant, once a racing epicenter equal to Ford's Holman-Moody works in Charlotte, had been expanded and modernized. Kyle Petty, now CEO of Petty Enterprises, made sure I saw the new engineering building, which looks much like a

"The King" didn't always wear that cowboy hat. He wore a beard for a short time in 1976 and sported other current fashions—a turtleneck, an open collar denim jacket, and glasses. Below he's in his late 1970s driver getup. *Dick Conway*

university research laboratory. I sat down with Richard again, in the same office we'd sat in years before, and again he talked as long as I wanted to listen.

Out of necessity, he had developed certain interview routines—offering his Arnold Palmer analogy (Arnold Palmer is to golf as Richard Petty is to racing) and referring to his wife Lynda's effort to be his number two priority, behind racing of course. You've seen these anecdotes in print before. They are points of reference, constantly updated and changing, chameleon-like, used by "The King" to expedite processes and to simplify life.

During our talk, he remembered showing up for a TV appearance in Nashville some years ago. "I didn't have my cowboy hat, didn't have my glasses on, and the cat said, 'What are you doing? Who are you?'

"Know what I mean?"

For many, Richard Petty would only be remembered for the look he adopted in the early- to mid-1970s—even though he was well-known during his young buck period in the early 1960s and when he matured to his Mario Andretti look (with coif and sunburns) around 1969. But in the last 20 years of his career, that image of him offering a big smile in a flamboyant cowboy hat (complete with feathers) became iconic.

"To some extent, you know, it's not *all* of Richard Petty, but it's the part of Richard Petty that shows up," he said during our conversation.

"So where's the real Richard Petty?" I asked.

"He's hid behind them glasses," he said without flinching.

Then "The King" flashed the characteristic Petty smile. "That's my security blanket, OK? I feel like if I've got the hat and glasses on, I can do and say what I want to. I can go hide a little bit."

Yes, those under the celebrity microscope need a little space in which to hide, and Richard Petty, again seeking balance, found it. Thing is, there was and is nothing false about the image he presented; never has been. Richard Petty always has been Richard Petty—what you see is what it *is*, no more, no less.

It's easy to let Richard Petty the personality overshadow Richard Petty the race car driver. The racing part seems so long ago, while the personality endures. The main point of this book will be to show, line-by-line and in Richard's own words, the racing part of his legacy. Without the racing—the skills and the records—none of the rest would have happened. Know what I mean? So OK, Richard, it's time to start talking . . .

After Petty won the first two Winston Cups, he became increasingly fond of heavyweight championship beltware, such as this 1972 title commemorative. The buckles gradually became part of the Petty look. *Dick Conway*

Petty hoists a special present from a fan at Charlotte. Petty received many such tokens of affection over his long career. *Dick Conway*

The greatest of their time: Cale Yarborough, in Junior Johnson's No. 11, outran Petty for championships in 1976, 1977, and 1978. "The King," however, returned to the top in 1979, edging Darrell Waltrip by 11 points. *Dick Conway*

Emerging star Dale Earnhardt (on the outside) eventually took the cape from "The King" as NASCAR's most-popular star. He made his full-time debut in 1979 and won rookie-of-the-year honors while Petty won his seventh, and final, championship. *Dick Conway*

Richard earned such a level of respect among fans that at one point "Petty for President" bumper stickers became commonplace. This one covers the bumper of a Plymouth at Daytona in 1980.
Dick Conway

CHAPTER ONE

THE BEGINNINGS OF A DYNASTY

——

"A farmer's son knows farming.
He don't go out and become a coach
or run a car dealership.
He stays within his field.
That's basically what I did."

I f you look way down the list of finishers in that first Daytona 500 in 1959, all the way down to 57th place, you'll find the name Richard Petty, who drove a 1957 Oldsmobile convertible that day and was out after eight laps.

As what was called a "sweepstakes" race at the time, the inaugural Daytona 500 was open to entrants from NASCAR's Grand National and Convertible divisions (back in the late 1950s, NASCAR maintained a separate championship division for soft-top cars). Young Richard, who had only received his father's permission to race late in 1958, qualified well enough at Daytona and started sixth, but the engine in his car smoked out early.

Certainly more than a few eyes were on Richard that day, only his 15th time on the competitive racing circuit. He had chosen the number 43 because it was the number that came right after his father's 42, and many of the 40,000 or so who attended the first Daytona 500 were well acquainted with Lee Petty and with his son's growing interest in the family's sport and business.

Richard had started to pester his father about driving as he approached his 21st birthday—July 2, 1958—but Lee Petty was reluctant to let his son get behind the wheel and compete in such a dangerous sport. He finally relented, though, when a dilemma arose over two possible races in one day—July 12, 1958. Lee was scheduled to run the Grand National at Asheville, North Carolina, and had an Olds ragtop slated for a Convertible event open at Columbia, South Carolina.

"Daddy was going to Asheville, and normally we would pick another driver to run the convertible. I told Daddy he ought to let me drive the car instead of going out and looking for someone else," Richard reflects.

The race was a 200-lap run on a half-mile dirt oval. Richard gathered up cousin Dale Inman and neighborhood pals Wade Thornburg and Kenny "Red" Myler and headed south down U.S. 220 to Columbia for his first shot behind the wheel of a race car.

"See, I had been working on cars, and Daddy had been winning championships, winning a bunch of races, so I thought I wanted to drive. I just said 'I might like to do this, like to try it.' We went to Columbia and run the race, and I told Dale, 'I think I'm going to like this.' "

At the race, Petty and his "crew" pitted down toward the track's first corner. "Fireball [Roberts] and Bob Wellborn had that race covered—I think I was five or six laps behind—but I finished sixth," Richard says.

Needless to say, Richard was hooked. "Driving a race car was a way I could express *me*. When you seen that race car run, that was Richard Petty," he says. "I was expressing things I couldn't do or express any other way. It's kind of weird. This wound up being what I wanted to do, my way of making a living. Once I got into it, basically it was all I knew.

"A farmer's son knows farming. He don't go out and become a coach or run a car dealership. He stays within his field. That's basically what I did."

Richard almost immediately hit the Grand National tour, accompanying his father and the family crew to Toronto, nearly 900 miles away in Canada, for his first true Grand

National start the next week. Apparently Lee Petty was pleased with his son's performance at Columbia, and he could not cool young Richard's enthusiasm. So before returning to home ground in the fall, the younger Petty had hit the northern hot spots at Buffalo, New York, and Belmar, New Jersey.

Richard recalls it as a sort of gypsy tour. "We went from week to week, race to race. All we were interested in was doing enough in this race to get enough money to get to the next race because there was no sponsorship money, no deal money," he says.

Richard and his father Lee tune up Richard's Plymouth in one of NASCAR's early tin garages, probably at Charlotte or Darlington. *International Motorsports Hall of Fame Archives*

International Motorsports Hall of
Fame Archives

THE PATRIARCH GETS HIS START

The roots of the Petty dynasty run deep—all the way back to the very beginning of what eventually became NASCAR racing. Lee Petty, who first started tooling under the hoods of Fords in the 1930s, had already been involved in several local races in North Carolina when Bill France organized the first new-model stock car race at Charlotte on June 19, 1949.

Petty, probably through his already established connections in Randolph County, acquired a gigantic Buick six-seater for the 200-lap race and drove it to the three-quarter-mile track 70 miles from Level Cross. There, in beautiful weather with high summer cumulus overhead, NASCAR spread its wings and flew for the first time.

Of course, few in the upper realms of media paid note to Petty—who was out after 105 laps—or any of the other competitors that day; even the local media wasn't that interested. Yes, a reported 13,000 spectators had turned out to watch the show, but stock car racing—in fact, *most* automobile racing—was considered to be a passing carnival, something that was here today, gone tomorrow.

Bill France, founder of NASCAR, was determined to change that view. Energetic and forceful, France decided that the path to long-term prosperity was to enforce a sound organization that, for one, dependably delivered a show as advertised and, secondly, dependably paid the competitors. France also insisted that the cars be factory stock—right off the floor, or right out of the driveway.

So in that 1949 season, the first year of the Strictly Stock era, Petty ran six of the eight scheduled races. And after the first one, the Charlotte event, Petty made a crucial decision—he wanted to leave behind the two-ton Buick and race a lighter car on the next go around. It was a strategic and somewhat-against-the-grain idea that eventually put him behind the wheel of a two-seat Plymouth business coupe.

With the Plymouth, Petty earned his first victory and $1,500 at Pittsburgh on September 18. He also earned two second-place finishes that year with the lighter car, placing second in the points standings by the end of the season, and pocketed $3,855 out of the purses. This wasn't a huge sum of money, even by 1949 rates, but enough to make shrewd Lee Petty believe he could make more money than he would lose in racing; over the years he became known as a grim, dogged competitor, determined to get his full fair share of the pie.

After another successful season in 1950, where he earned $7,695 after winning the season-ender at Hillsboro, North Carolina, Lee was ready for another full year on the circuit. And his sons, Richard, almost 13, and Maurice, 11, really started to take an interest in what Dad was doing in the garage.

"He had a car, he put a number on it, he was a race car driver," Richard recalls. "He did all the fine mechanical work as far as tuning the thing up, setting up the steering, and so on. We could change oil, . . . could wash the thing, [and] change tires—same stuff any kid does in the driveway. That's where we started.

"When we got old enough, we drove 'em to the racetrack or towed 'em to the racetrack. Then [we started] pitting the cars."

Maybe only the Wood Brothers, who became the Pettys' fiercest rivals in the 1960s and 1970s, grew so organically, as if out of the soil. Lee Petty was a racer, and the family—sons, cousins, wives, mothers—gathered around and became part of it.

After switching to Dodges and Chryslers in 1954, Lee won his first Grand National championship and reported a season take of $21,127, making Petty Enterprises a bonafide successful business.

In all, he spent 12 years as a full-time driver, becoming the first to win three NASCAR championships (in 1954, 1958, and 1959). Now, 50 years later, only three other drivers have surpassed that feat—his son Richard, who won the all-time record of seven; Dale Earnhardt, who shares that seven-victory record; and Jeff Gordon, who has won four titles. Only three more have equaled Lee Petty's mark—David Pearson, Cale Yarborough, and Darrell Waltrip.

Perhaps Petty's most memorable contribution to NASCAR was in the launch of NASCAR's second era, which began at France's gigantic new Daytona International Speedway on February 22, 1959. The new track—an entirely new concept, 2.5 miles around and high-banked in the corners—scared a lot of the racers, accustomed as they were to flat half-miles. But Lee Petty was not frightened; he joined 58 other brave men for that first Daytona 500, which remarkably was run without a caution.

He started 15th in the race, driving a white, No. 42 Oldsmobile, and took the lead for the first time on lap 150 of 200. He battled Iowa driver Johnny Beauchamp to the finish, and they crossed the line dead-even.

NASCAR officials initially declared Beauchamp the winner, escorting him to the trophy celebration. Petty and his supporters believed otherwise, and there was enough uproar for the sanction to begin a review. NASCAR officials apparently played the commotion for all it was worth, taking nearly three days to reach a decision, in which they declared Lee Petty the winner, thus giving Petty a dramatic imprint on the subsequent history of the sport.

By the beginning of the 1960s, Lee's lineage in the sport started to become even more established, as his business was flourishing, he was a multichampion driver, and 21-year-old Richard was becoming the newest racing phenom.

Lee Petty in the seat of one of the Carl Kiekhaefer Chrysler 300s. Petty never drove for Kiekhaefer, but his relationship with Chrysler had begun to flourish by the time this photo was taken in 1955. *International Motorsports Hall of Fame Archives*

Lee Petty steers his lightweight Plymouth coupe through the turn at Martinsville as Slick Smith's Hudson veers toward the fence. *International Motorsports Hall of Fame Archives*

There have been whispers, though, that Lee Petty had established at least an informal relationship with Oldsmobile officials and the marque's dealer network in 1957, resulting in the changeover from Chrysler to Olds. Richard brushes off those rumors, insisting, "Daddy was footing the bill. We didn't have dealerships behind us. Racing was all we done, racing was our livelihood. If we didn't make [money], we didn't go to the next race, or we didn't eat, or whatever it was, and everybody struggled."

As the 1959 season approached, Lee Petty decided to run two cars full time on the Grand National circuit. He would run his own No. 42 Oldsmobile and provide the No. 43 for Richard. Richard, years later, still wasn't quite sure how it all came to be.

"At the time, he was forty-five years old. I never talked to him about it, so I don't know what his whole take on the deal was," Richard says. "I guess he thought, 'I can't do this forever, and if the only business we got is the racing business, we're going to have to have another driver, so why not keep it in the family.' "

Richard's natural talent was immediately apparent in those early races. He instantly became comfortable behind the wheel, just as if he were a fish that had been dropped back into his native waters. He was exactly where he belonged, where he would stay until that bittersweet final day at Atlanta in November 1992, 33 seasons later.

Where it all started: These are seldom-seen images of the one-time junk lot behind the Petty compound at Level Cross, which was visible as late as 1983. The rusty Plymouth in the background appears to have had its number altered from 42 to 43. The car in the foreground, if you look closely, shows the name "Richard" scratched into the dashboard. *Dick Conway*

No one really knew the importance of Lee Petty's biggest catch until the Martinsville race in May, in which Richard finished seventh and Lee won by five laps over Johnny Beauchamp. Then on June 14, both Pettys competed at Atlanta's odd-shaped Lakewood Speedway dirt track, in a race that has become part of this racing family's legendary history.

Richard crossed the finish line first, went to the trophy circle, and everything. Lee finished second and immediately headed to the scoring stand to demand a recheck of cards. An hour later, officials declared that Lee Petty, not Richard Petty, was the winner of the race. Father hence deprived son of his first victory. Lee's reasoning, stated at the time, was that if his son intended to win races, he'd better be prepared to win them fair and square and be ready to defend what had been won.

Nevertheless, by the end of 1959, both Pettys had something to cheer, with Lee winning his third Grand National championship (then a record, waiting to be broken by his son) and Richard winning rookie-of-the-year honors after competing in 21 of 44 races and finishing six times in the top five.

Richard won his first-ever race of any kind that fall, in a Convertible run, at Columbia. Convertible races do not count in the Grand National records, although Richard recalls the race with pride because he competed against some of NASCAR's best that day.

"I drove a '59 Plymouth," he says. "I beat Jack Smith on the last lap—me and [legendary car owner] Bud Moore were talking about that. That was my first win, but that don't count. So the first race I won was February [1960] at the old Charlotte Fairgrounds."

Another look at where old race cars were sent to die. On a winter day in North Carolina, these rusting hulks lay as relics in the founding of a dynasty. *Dick Conway*

On the hard sand at Daytona, Lee with his car and trophy after being declared the winner of the 1954 beach race. Tim Flock finished first, but was disqualified. This was Petty's only win on the beach, and it launched him toward the 1954 championship. *International Motorsports Hall of Fame Archives*

As it turned out, Lee Petty turned the Atlanta disfavor into a favor at the Charlotte event, another signpost in Petty lore. At the February 28, 1960, race, Richard passed Maryland driver Rex White on the 182nd of 200 laps. Lee Petty, who had taken over in relief of Doug Yates after his own car failed on the 39th lap, bumped White as Rex tried to regain the lead on Lap 187, helping Richard to get away clean.

National Speed Sport News, the longtime bible of motorsports, noted the event under this headline: "Charlotte GN to Dick Petty." The account further stated:

> For young Dick Petty, NASCAR's stylish-driving rookie of the year in 1959, it was an initial victory in the Grand National circuit ranks for a late-model hardtop race. He had posted a convertible win at Columbia South Carolina, prior to Sunday's triumph, which came after his sixth start here.
>
> The younger Petty, [who is] rapidly developing into one of the NASCAR circuit's finest drivers, also had a boost from his dad, Lee Petty, at the 187th lap as the hard-charging White came on again in a strong bid to

In what must have been a posed shot, Richard (right) takes aim with a hammer while brother Maurice, in a typical tinkering pose, stares under the hood. *International Motorsports Hall of Fame Archives*

regain the lead. Lee Petty—who had Yates' Plymouth right up with the leaders, although not into same lap contention—bore in on White at the first turn causing a near spinout.

With White falling back momentarily in the Chevy, the younger Petty took a commanding lead that he never relinquished. Asked if he thought he's helped his son to win by his maneuver, the former triple national champion smiled, "Maybe I didn't help him, but I sure didn't hurt him any."

That was win number 1, and 199 would follow. "I never even thought about it that way," Richard recalls. "We just went from week to week."

Richard won two other races that year, at Martinsville in the spring and at Hillsboro, North Carolina, in the fall. These added to an altogether successful season for Petty Enterprises, fulfilling Lee Petty's gamble on his son, who finished second in points to Rex White and earned $41,873. The elder Petty earned sixth place in the standings that year, winning five times and collecting $31,282.

Bear in mind that the money figures reported here are spurious, as NASCAR payouts always have been suspect. Until recently, phony money was often included in these figures, even though it was not always paid out if a driver did not participate in certain events. The

Richard's Plymouth shows battle scars as he guides it off a turn during a dirt-track race in the late 1960s. Attendance then wasn't what it is today. *International Motorsports Hall of Fame Archives*

numbers above are on the high end, with other sources reporting much lower numbers—Richard making $17,228 and Lee $14,510. Still other sources report that Richard pocketed $35,180 and Lee $26,650. We'll leave the differences to the scholars. At either end, the take was pretty good in 1960 dollars.

The emerging dream team, however, crashed to earth early in 1961, as the season opened at Daytona. Richard qualified to start in the 14th spot in the first twin heat. But on the 38th lap (of 40), Junior Johnson lost control of his Pontiac and rapped the side of Petty's Plymouth, sending Richard into a wild spin and actually out of the park, into a muddy lot off Turn 1. Petty suffered bruises to his face and a cut hand; he was lucky.

Far worse was Lee Petty's crash in the second twin. It coincidentally happened while racing against Johnny Beauchamp—his mate in the 1959 Daytona 500 dead heat. Petty's car and Beauchamp's car locked bumpers in Turn 3, with both cars vaulting the guardrail and landing in heaps.

Lee's injuries, as reported, included a punctured lung, broken ribs, a broken thigh, a broken collarbone, and multiple internal injuries. The three-time champion was immediately hospitalized and remained there, enduring a painful recovery, for four months. Meanwhile, Beauchamp faced recovering from head injuries. Because of the crash, neither he nor Lee Petty seriously raced again.

Richard did not compete in the Daytona 500 that year—one of only two Daytona 500s among the first 45 to be run without a Petty in the field (the second was in 1965, when the Pettys stood aside due to the Chrysler boycott of NASCAR). He, along with Maurice, Dale, Wade, and Red, went home to take stock.

The following summer was the darkest period in the history of Petty Enterprises. "We had some rough years, but '61 was terrible," Richard recalls. "[Daddy] crashed at Daytona, I crashed at Daytona, we just had two cars. When I came home, there wasn't nothing. He was in the hospital for four months. I was twenty-three years old, Chief [Maurice] was twenty-one or twenty-two.

"Mother had always kept the books, and Daddy had always done all the mechanical deals or told us what to do. Now all the sudden, we were having to keep the books, do the bank account—that kind of fell on me. You work during the day, then you get up all the bills that come down at night. . . . I was looking after all the finances, what little they were, and trying to figure out if we had enough money to buy tires or go to the next race."

At that critical moment, Richard Petty became the leader this racing family rallied behind.

"It was probably one of the better things from my standpoint, to make me understand," he says. "I grew up real quick. I was a twenty-three-year-old kid. Daddy had been taking care of everything, and all the sudden *you've* got to take care of everything. You've got to start making decisions yourself, and the whole family, financial-wise, is throwed on you. So all the sudden, you grow up real, real quick."

Soon Richard and Maurice gathered up enough capital to acquire another Plymouth locally, just to keep going to the next week. "We went to town, bought a car, brought it

Up to speed: At right Petty passes Red
Foote on the outside during the 1962
World 600 at Charlotte. He's challenging
Larry Thomas below. "The King" led the
race twice, for five laps, but finished fourth.
Bob Tronolone

This is what "stock" cars looked like in the early 1960s. Here Petty coasts in his 1962 Plymouth to the pits. Note minimal alterations to the body and frame structure on the car.
Bob Tronolone

back, worked on it," Richard says. "We had terrible luck that year, engines breaking—of course I was building the engines. But the alternative was folding up the family in racing. We never thought about doing anything but what we was doing. We had a one-track mind. In the latter part of '61, we finally got our stuff together."

Petty won just two races that year, at Richmond and at Charlotte in late spring, and he finished eighth in points.

He and his brother's involvement in the company, and Pop's return to the front office, started paying off in 1962. Lee even ran one race that year, finishing fifth in the spring 500 at Martinsville, perhaps just to be sure he still could compete. Maurice pitched in behind the wheel and did not do badly at all, running nine races in 1961 and five in 1962.

Richard, meanwhile, turned up the wick, winning eight times in 1962 and finishing in the top five in 32 of his 52 starts. His total take (again, sources vary) was $60,763.

As early as 1953, Lee Petty had begun to field extra cars to cover fair-paying races he couldn't make himself. Sportsman champion Ralph Earnhardt, father of Dale, was one of his early retainers, running eight races in Petty cars in 1957. Bob Welborn, from nearby Denton, North Carolina, and Jim Paschal, from High Point, were dependable favorites. With Lee sidelined, Paschal was enlisted in late summer of 1962 to drive the No. 42 car, and he promptly ripped off three victories in a row—at Bristol, Nashville, and Asheville. Paschal also bucked up the team in 1963, winning five times in 29 starts for Petty Enterprises—just over half the season.

The 1963 campaign became the best yet for Richard and for Petty Enterprises. Richard won 14 races, which, including Paschal's five, gave the group 19 wins in 95 entries. The Pettys also put out cars for Maurice, Welborn, Jim Hurtubise, Bob James, Jimmy Massey, and even Joe Weatherly, who was "hitchhiking" his way to the championship. He drove for eight different car owners that year, most often for Bud Moore, before winning the 1963 title.

Little did Lee Petty know when he first started racing that someday his family would run a racing empire, one that has been involved in the stock car world for 50-plus years. *Bob Tronolone*

Lee, the patriarch, and Richard share a smile during the era that Richard's career was sizzling—the 1970s. During that decade, he won five driving championships and bolstered his win total to 190. *Halifax Historical Society (Daytona Beach, Florida) Collection*

By the middle of 1963, Petty Enterprises arguably had become the premier organization in NASCAR, a fast turnabout from the dark nights of February and March 1961. Petty cars, even the cast-offs and "team" cars, were considered potential winners at any stop, and the team had begun to receive unofficial support from Chrysler, as the Detroit works opened its eyes to stock car racing and geared up toward broader involvement in the sport.

All of these factors were in play as Daytona approached in 1964, the beginning of the most tumultuous stretch of time in NASCAR history.

Three stalwarts: Richard has a positive word with crew chief and cousin Dale Inman. Looking on from the right is Buddy Parrott, who went on to build a legend of his own and served as crew chief for Petty's 199th and 200th victories. *Dick Conway*

CHAPTER TWO

DAYTONA AND THE HEMI HELP DEFINE NASCAR

—

"So you look at Daytona,
and you look at Richard Petty's career,
they went together.
I was fortunate enough to win a bunch of races,
and as Daytona was growing in prestige,
I kept growing with prestige."

In 1964, two major developments made Richard Petty's career soar: He won the Daytona 500 and the Hemi engine became the powerplant for his Chrylser.

". . . At the time, Darlington was still the biggest thing. Darlington was here; Daytona was just another race, but it kept doing one of these deals," he says, raising and lowering his hands like a scale balancing. "In '59, '60, and '61, Daytona's prestige had been growing.

"It was the perfect time to have a race—nobody's been racing for three months, so it's the beginning of the racing season for everybody, and all the racing people all over the world look at Daytona to crank up another year."

"So you look at Daytona, and you look at Richard Petty's career, they went together. I was fortunate enough to win a bunch of races, and as Daytona was growing in prestige, I kept growing with prestige."

Bill France was the mastermind behind Daytona. He had seen how successful the Southern 500 had become, and by as early as 1954, when the Southern 500 at Darlington had become the second largest motorsports race, France envisioned creating the Daytona speedway. His dream became a reality in 1959. Soon other promoters tried to bank on his genius, but failed; Bruton Smith and Curtis Turner bankrupted themselves in building the Charlotte Motor Speedway (now Lowe's Motor Speedway) in 1960, and a consequent controversy over a proposed million-dollar loan from the national Teamsters Union resulted in an effort to "unionize" racing drivers.

Big, modern speedways eventually went up at Atlanta and at Rockingham, North Carolina, the Rockingham track being built by the same speculators—a group of land manipulators and drinking buddies—who had built Darlington. Toward the middle of the decade, a Detroit speculator named Larry LoPatin set out to build massive new tracks in Michigan's Irish Hills (now Michigan International Speedway), in Texas, and in New Jersey. In a few short years, racing had jumped from a highlight of the county fair to big business. And that's exactly where Richard Petty came in.

"You look back, you look at NASCAR, you look at Richard Petty. Richard Petty grew up with NASCAR," "The King" says. "We went the same scale. We went up the hill together. There again, I was thrown in that position to be the one that come along with it."

In one of his favorite analogies, Richard compares his career with that of golfer Arnold Palmer.

"He had everything. He had Arnie's army. He was the man. So he took golf out of the dark ages, took 'em off the back page, and put 'em on the front page—same way Tiger [Woods] done.

"You read the paper today . . . and Tiger is fourteen strokes behind, but he gets his name in there. They done the same thing with Arnie; he was the leader. I was thrown into that situation. I was sort of the lead deal. I couldn't do it myself without all the other guys, and they beat me sometimes and I beat them sometimes. But when the press came or the people came, they would think, 'There's *the guy*'—sort of like Earnhardt [Dale Earnhardt Jr.] is now, whether he runs third or last or whatever.

"He's throwed in that position, partly because of what he is, but also because of what his dad had done. If his dad was Dale Jones, he would have been just another [driver]. So I did the same thing in following my father. The Petty name was already out there. Any hard-core racing fan knew the Petty name. So I added a little bit bigger front name and just took it to the next level."

Part of that next level had to do with the brutishly powerful Hemi engine. Detroit, after a turbulent (and not always observed) seven-year layoff from official sanctioning in stock car racing, took off the gloves in 1962. In 1964, when Ford returned with a full-fledged

Petty guides his unmarked Plymouth to the finish line for his first Daytona 500 victory, one of seven for "The King." He finished more than a lap ahead of second-place Jimmy Pardue. *International Motorsports Hall of Fame Archives*

Father Lee Petty shares the spotlight with his son at Daytona. Even after 500 miles, Richard seems not to have a hair out of place. On the left is Ronney Householder, head of Chrysler's racing effort. *International Motorsports Hall of Fame Archives*

effort, Chrysler turned out the most tremendous of the 1960s muscle car powerplants just in time for the that season's Daytona 500: the fabled 426 ci with hemispherical combustion chambers—the Hemi, as unholy a piece of American metal as ever left an assembly line.

The impact of the Hemi has been lost in time, with today's tightly controlled box-stock engines routinely turning out 900 horsepower and 10,000 rpm. The Hemi was basically a factory piece (very few of them even turned up in street cars) that produced 400 horsepower (depending on carburetion) and fit in a lightweight Plymouth Belvedere body and frame.

The engine seemed to catch Bill France by surprise. In opening test runs at Daytona, the Mopar/Hemi cars, led by Richard Petty, were 10 miles per hour faster than anything else on the track. So when you get down to it, Petty was sitting on the biggest bull in the yard and riding it to the limit.

"I don't know when they officially announced they were racing," Petty says of Chrysler, "but we had been operating with them under the table since the middle of '59. In '61, '62, it got to be a little more. In '63, the company started modifying the wedge motor. It didn't let us know, but engineers were already working on the Hemi. Junior [Johnson] went to

What it's all about: Petty salutes the crowd after his big win. The man in the glasses to the right of Richard is Bill France Sr. Lee Petty is on the far right. *International Motorsports Hall of Fame Archives*

In the days before reliable radios, drivers cued their teams via signals, or merely by trying to shout over the engine. Richard attempts to instruct his crew during a tire stop.

International Motorsports Hall of Fame Archives

Maurice (note the boots) drags the gun and hose to the left side of the car after servicing the right side. Sticker tires are on the right; the jack man is a little behind. *International Motorsports Hall of Fame Archives*

the test track in Arizona, tested the Dodge, tested the Hemi, the whole deal. Then they came back and said, 'OK guys, this is what we got this year.' And there we went.

"It was unreal, even at the time. Chevrolet was in and out of racing, Pontiac was in and out, and they both had racing engines. We didn't have the racing parts. In the latter part of '63, [Chrysler] started making the heads, some stuff for that particular engine, then the company just busted loose with the whole engine. That caught Ford—that caught everybody—flat-footed."

The Hemi helped power Richard Petty to his first Daytona 500 win in 1964, which came despite frantic attempts by Bill France to reel in the engine that knocked everything

out of orbit and set off a stretch of increasingly contentious boycotts and competitive innovations for the rest of the decade. In the coming years, this engine put France at the center of the volcano, where he felt forced to block this part and that, as well as make new rules for a burgeoning sport.

Richard won nine races with the Hemi that first season, not as many as he had in 1963, but he did capture his first Grand National championship, running away from 1961 champ Ned Jarrett, who won 15 races. In those days, money counted in the points standings, and Petty's Daytona win helped put him over the top, with a season total of $114,771.45.

The Pettys weren't the only ones who were triumphant that 1964 season—Jarrett had a good year, as did the emerging South Carolina hot rod David Pearson, and Fred Lorenzen, a Chicago superstar who won half the races he entered (8 of 16).

One of the common sights in the track infields during the 1970s and 1980s was a second-hand school bus that was decked out in the colors of the owner's favorite driver. Here a Petty fan offers his homage to "The King" at Daytona. *Dick Conway*

Richard, in the STP Dodge, leads Buddy Baker's Ford down the front side at the Daytona 500 in 1977. Baker, a top dog on the big tracks, drove three-plus years for Bud Moore. *Dick Conway*

Yet it had been terribly tragic year in other ways. Popular Joe Weatherly died in a crash at Riverside in January (he was the first NASCAR driver to die in seven years) and the effect was stunning. Then, in May at Charlotte, Glenn "Fireball" Roberts was badly burned in a crash early in the World 600; he suffered for a month in a hospital, then died. And, in September, Jimmy Pardue was killed during a suicidal tire test at Charlotte. So fate, triumph, and tragedy therefore seemed to pitch unassuming young Richard Petty into a role that year—a role NASCAR fans always seem to seek and find. The best comparisons of this phenomenon may be to the 1993 and 2001 seasons, with comparable circumstances more familiar to present NASCAR observers.

In 1993, two of NASCAR's top idols died. Alan Kulwicki, underdog champion in 1992, was killed in a plane crash near Bristol, Tennessee, on April Fools' Day that year. In July, beloved Davey Allison, horsing around with his new helicopter at the Talladega speedway, crashed and died the next morning. These were dark days for NASCAR. The talent pipeline had produced only aging campaigners such as Dick Trickle and Jimmy Hensley, and two of the biggest stars were down.

Enter Jeff Gordon.

In 2001, Dale Earnhardt, successor to Richard Petty as the greatest racer of a quarter-century, died in a crash on the last lap of the Daytona 500. That followed a disastrous 2000, during which Adam Petty and Kenny Irwin were killed in wrecks at the New Hampshire International Speedway.

Enter Dale Earnhardt Jr.

Both these references give an idea of what NASCAR needed—and what NASCAR *found*—as 1964 turned to 1965. Richard Petty, his tanned face eternally smiling in the slanting sunlight of victory lane, was the champion—a man made for this time and this time made for this man.

The Petty team rolls its Buick into victory lane at Daytona after the 1981 Daytona 500, which turned out to be the last of Richard's seven wins in the big race. He won 500s in four different car makes. *Dick Conway*

CHAPTER THREE

THE STREAK CEMENTS THE ULTIMATE SEASON

———

"Just to run every lap in ten races in a row
is a pretty good feat,
and we did it for two months.
As we were doing it,
we'd come home, get ready for the next race—
you didn't think about adding it up."

The triumph and tragedy of the 1964 racing season turned to tumult in 1965, and again Richard Petty was in the middle of it. Now the sport's biggest star, Petty (as well as his team) had been adopted by Chrysler Corporation as the company's lead player in stock car racing.

The problem was that Chrysler and the other car companies involved in racing (Ford had its shop set up in Charlotte at the fabled Holman-Moody works) were coming under greater scrutiny after the deaths of three top competitors in 1964. These tragedies had raised awareness that the cars being used in the sport were not safe at the speeds possible on the new speedways, and Bill France realized that his original vision for *stock* car racing was not going to work in the brave new world of NASCAR. Cars would need to be modified—to move in the direction of becoming *race* cars.

As part of that, cars began to be constructed differently, on unibody platforms but with a sturdier front frame. Then the auto companies started using rubber-lined fuel cells, derived from the tank bladders used in fighter planes, on the cars. These cells were made up of a thick rubber liner encased in a steel box, a setup that could resist puncture much better than a standard gas tank under a trunk. Better tires made their way onto the refurbished cars, and these had an inner liner, creating almost a tire within a tire. With this liner, the tire would hold up if the outer liner was punctured or if it lost pressure, thus preventing a catastrophic blowout.

Richard keeps his eyes on the track ahead during the 1966 season, when he finished third in the points race. *Mike Smith Photography (www.turboracingphotos.com)*

But for Chrysler, the biggest car design change came when Bill France and other NASCAR officials wanted to address engine horsepower, which now allowed cars to reach up to 160 miles per hour. At the obvious center of that issue was the Chrysler Hemi. After considering its options for weeks, the group offered its verdict before Christmas 1964: The Hemi would not be allowed in NASCAR in 1965, and the Chrysler teams would be required to run the heavy Plymouth Fury and Dodge Polara cars.

That sent a shudder through the Chrysler camp, and despite the company's repeated politicking in Daytona, nothing had changed by the 1965 season's opening. Chrysler officials therefore shook hands politely with Bill France and advised their racers to go elsewhere. The boycott was on. Some of Chrysler's top dogs were advised to race in the lower-paying USAC stock series, where the Hemi was still legal.

"Y'all go drag racing until we get all this politics squared away," Richard remembers Chrysler execs saying when they informed him of the boycott. And that's exactly what he and his team did. After July 1965, NASCAR allowed a compromise in which Hemis could run on shorter tracks.

"We could still run the Hemi, but it had to be a [track of a] mile or below. So we got to run some of the short tracks, got to run Rockingham [in October]. That was the only big race we ran that year. [Chrysler] didn't want to lose what we already had built up in '64, so the company had to keep me out there," he adds. "The next year, NASCAR just cut the cubic inches down to four hundred and five. We went to Daytona and still blowed 'em away."

Richard checks out the systems in his car before the start at Riverside in 1967. The No. 43, finally standardized with STP in 1972, was still evolving. *Bob Tronolone*

Petty guns his Plymouth through Turn 6 at Riverside in 1967. The race took two weeks to run, with rain on January 22 forcing the conclusion of the race to be run on January 29. In the end, Parnelli Jones won it. *Bob Tronolone*

Petty's all smiles in his Plymouth at Daytona. *International Motorsports Hall of Fame Archives*

Petty didn't start off his monumental 1967 season with a win at Riverside, but that didn't matter. He still won 27 races that year, 10 of those consecutively. *Mike Smith Photography (www.turboracingphotos.com)*

The drag racing interlude was curious, and in the end tragic. Richard, driving a No. 43 Jr. Plymouth Barracuda with the word "Outlawed" scribed on the side, actually won the meet at Bristol, Tennessee, during his brief tenure on the hot rod circuit. However, in February, at a primitive quarter-mile outside Atlanta, Petty's car mechanically failed and veered into the close-gathered crowd, vaulting a dirt berm. A wheel broke off, hitting and killing an eight-year-old boy.

Even after 40 years, and dozens of other racing highlights and lowlights, Richard would rather not talk about that day. The tragic Georgia drag race "was not a pretty situation," he says quietly. "That was probably the downest I've ever been—up until '75, when my brother-in-law [Randy Owens] was killed at Talladega. Those were the two lowest points because you were directly involved."

"Yet I'm a strong believer in mind over matter," he further explains. "It's like when we lost Adam [in 2000]. Everything just stopped here. We did, so they [Petty Enterprises employees] did. Then you set down one day and say, 'We're still here. We've got our family, we've got all these families. We've got to keep this deal going.' So you've got to work your way back out of it."

Petty ended up competing in 14 NASCAR races toward the end of 1965, after NASCAR officials begged the successful and fan favorite king to return, and he won four times. Ned Jarrett claimed the season championship.

In 1966, Chrysler and France made an uneasy peace, with NASCAR allowing the Hemi on short and intermediate tracks, and adding a weight handicap on the big tracks. Aggressive Ford, however, pulled a surprise out of the bag, offering its 427-ci overhead-cam engine to the sanction. France balked, insisting on a weight handicap for the Ford engine this time around. And like Chrysler in 1965, Ford pulled out in a huff, not returning until the fall, when France (under pressure from several ingenious competitors) realized he needed to compromise his terms.

Petty won 8 of 39 races that year and finished third in points. The new points champion was a 31-year-old from South Carolina, David Pearson, who was starting to become Petty's greatest rival.

The next year, 1967, cemented Richard Petty's place in racing history, and every NASCAR fan young enough not to remember that year wants to know how it became the greatest single season by any single driver—anywhere, anytime—the year that made Richard Petty "*The King.*" Yet Richard, honestly, does not have a lot of answers.

"We had the same cars [as in 1966], the same motors, the same workers, the same amount of money to work with, the whole deal. It just fell together," he says.

In fact, it *was* the same car, or at least the same car model, the team ran in 1966. It had been disguised, though, after Petty and his team lost the Daytona 500 to Mario Andretti, to look like a retrimmed 1967 Belvedere. After that move, initiated by brilliant crew chief Maurice Petty, the season took off.

As war flared in Asia, Clapton became God, and America saw society change big time, Richard Petty's racing career rose to dizzy heights. Still today Petty's statistics from that year are unbelievable. He won 27 of 48 races (56.3 percent, never approached by a driver running the full season), and he won 10 in a row (again, a record that will not be touched; four in a row seems to be the limit). With those kind of numbers, it was as if Petty had tapped into Olympic greatness, where the gods roamed the garages and the racetrack. The odd irony was that Petty never let his pride become an Achilles' heel; he remained an ultimately modest and approachable man. He continued to spend time with his fans, often signing scraps of paper, hats, shirts, breasts, for three or four hours, until his handlers dragged him away.

What happened that year happened, and Richard shrugs and accepts it. He is as much in awe of it as the rest of the racing world is.

"We went to Nashville, a little half-mile track, blew a tire, tore the whole back end off the car. The front end was all out of line," Petty says. "We came into the pits, [and] Dale lines up the front end just on sight, and the car's running good. The big deal is [that] somebody's got like a twelve-lap lead. They fell out; then somebody's got like a ten-lap lead. They fell out. So four or five guys are in front of us, and they fell out. We kept on trucking and wound up winning the cotton-picking race.

"That was in that ten-race deal. You can't explain stuff like that. You just went and did what you could. No matter what the circumstances, you tried and got the best out of it. That's the kind of year it was. Just to run every lap in ten races in a row is a pretty good feat, and we did it for *two months.* As we were doing it, we'd come home, get ready for the next race—you didn't think about adding it up.

Petty Blue became a popular color on all kinds of gadgets and garments once Richard became the winningest driver in racing. One fan painstakingly decided to paint this folding chair as a tribute to "The King." *Dick Conway*

In the 1960s and early 1970s, "official" driver shirts and jackets were not quite that official yet. This fan, like many others at the time, decided to create her own. *Dick Conway*

Petty steers a very clean, well-prepared Plymouth past a grandstand full of fans ready to see a legend in action at Riverside in the late 1960s. Note the smoke coming from either the brakes or tires on his car. *Bob Tronolone*

In the early days of NASCAR, before there were radios, this list reflected how drivers signaled to their pit crews. Holding up one, two, and three fingers asked for tires, oil, or water, respectively. If a driver banged on the roof, he was signaling that the car was pushing. If he banged on the door, the car was loose. *Dick Conway*

"All the sudden, you'd read about it in the paper. The press had picked up on it then, and they really took that and made a big deal of it. Plymouth took us to New York and had a big press conference. Nobody'd heard about it up there. They took us up there in front of the national media, New York media, or whatever. So that was another breakout for NASCAR.

"The greatest thing out of that whole deal was some guy up there in Canada sent us a little clip . . . maybe two or three paragraphs. I guess it was in the sports section. It said Petty runs second at some race, and it don't even tell who won the race. It [went on about] Petty having trouble and this is the reason why he run second and didn't even tell who won the cotton-picking race. That's when the press was really in a Tiger Woods [type of] deal."

As a result of Petty's success, and his being the right man for the right time, the sport of NASCAR grew.

"[That year] broke us out of the South," he recalls, still amazed. "Those people in Canada, California were paying attention to this because it was out of the ordinary, beyond the call of duty. They didn't know nothing about it, but this [campaign] was a special deal."

Almost forgotten amid the commotion over "The Streak" and the resulting championship was that Petty became the sport's all-time leading winner in 1967, surpassing his father, the prior leader. Richard's victory at Darlington in May was his 55th. Lee Petty had won his 54th (and last) at Jacksonville, Florida, in 1961, when no one really was counting. And by the end of 1967, Richard had racked up 75 of his 200 career wins.

Richard also turned 30 that year, and his nickname, "The King," became an integral part of his legend. Four decades later, it lives on. Even Richard's son Kyle calls him that.

Petty, like everyone else on the team, pitched in with the grunt work at the track. He never hesitated to do tasks like rolling tires to the hauler after a rain-out. Here, he's at Richmond in 1979. *Dick Conway*

As for how he got to be known as "The King," Petty credits the press with popularizing the moniker. "I think there was a clique of reporters—Jim Hunter, Bob Moore, Bob Myers, Benny Phillips, Joe Whitlock. The first thing they came up with was 'The Silver Fox' [for David Pearson]. Then they wrote 'King Richard,' and everybody takes it up, so then it just snowballs.

"I told those guys, 'If my name had been Joe, what would you have called me?' It wouldn't have been 'King Joe.' My name was Richard, so it went right with it. It could have been 'King David' [Pearson], but they already had him as 'The Silver Fox.' "

In next decade, "The King" and "The Silver Fox" became fierce competitors on the track—they battled it out more times than most would care to count. Each step of the way their rivalry deepened, becoming the greatest standing duel in NASCAR history.

CHAPTER FOUR

"THE KING" AND "THE SILVER FOX" BATTLE IT OUT

———

"When we got in a race car,
we both looked at racing the same way.
We don't care who leads the race,
we just want to win—
whatever it takes to get the job done."

David Gene Pearson was from upcountry South Carolina, 200-some miles southwest of the Pettys' Level Cross home base. His hometown of Whitney was in an area along the red-clay Piedmont axis that connected the racing centers of Richmond, Greensboro, Charlotte, Spartanburg, and Atlanta. Pearson, like Petty, was born to race; three years older than Petty, he actually preceded the budding stock car king in the cockpit by a few years, making his first jalopy start at a South Carolina dirt track in 1953.

Before that time, no other racers were like these legends, and none have been like them since. Fans lined up fervently to greet one or the other all the time, especially after Pearson became the flag carrier for Ford in 1968, with the enormous Ford factory team, which was run by the Holman-Moody works in Charlotte. Yet even before that, Pearson was beloved—a legion appreciated his pure racing ability so much that fans helped get "The Silver Fox" his first Grand National ride in 1960 partly as a result of a club vote, and then he went on to win the rookie-of-the-year title.

In 1963 Pearson started driving Everett "Cotton" Owens' No. 6 Dodges. Owens had built a Chrysler-backed powerhouse in the decade, fielding cars for Pearson, Darel Dieringer, Pete Hamilton, and others. Pearson won 27 of his 105 victories in Cotton's cars.

In 1967, Ford, realizing Pearson's genius, lured him to the Holman-Moody compound, preponderant rival to Petty's Chrysler effort. That move set off two fabulous racing seasons. Pearson won championships in 1968 and 1969, winning 27 races and 26 poles, as well as a half million dollars. Having also won the championship in 1966, he now was a step ahead of Petty, with three season trophies to Petty's two (Richard won in 1964 and 1967).

As the rivalry between Pearson and Petty continued to heat up those years, the contrasts between them became obvious. Pearson was stoic, silent, and down to business. Petty was out front and at ease with everyone. Pearson lurked in the shadows—seventh, eighth place—until it was time to go, and then he *went*. Petty was the colonel at the head of the gallant cavalry charge.

Pearson raced the full campaign in only four years, his career lasting from 1960 to 1986, when he abruptly snuffed it out, citing back pain and tiresome disputes with owners. He made his last big-time start in 1986. Except for a few years in the mid- to late-1960s, David never seemed to be exactly *in* the racing world, but instead somehow *above* it.

Many argue that Pearson's career stats are better than Petty's. In some ways, that's true. Pearson ran just less than half the races Petty did—574 to Petty's record 1,184. Of those, Pearson won 105, and Petty a record 200. You can figure the percentages: David Pearson won a little more than 18 percent of the time, Richard Petty just more than 17 percent of the time. Pearson is still second on the all-time wins list; no one comes even close to his numbers.

Pearson's standout 1973 season, which had possibilities of exceeding Richard's 1967 triumph, came while he was driving for the Wood Brothers. You have to clench your fists just thinking how good it was. Pearson and the Woods ran just 18 races and blew up in four of them—clutch at Riverside, engine at Daytona, differential at Martinsville, wreck at

Longtime rivals Richard Petty and David Pearson listen in with Bruce Hill, the 1975 rookie of the year, at the pre-race drivers meeting at Martinsville in the fall of 1975. *Dick Conway*

Petty and Pearson had vastly different personalities. Pearson was stoic, silent, and down to business. Petty was out front and at ease with everyone—always ready to ink his famous signature. He says he learned early on to sign from the elbow so as to avoid writer's cramp. *Dick Conway*

Charlotte. Of the remaining 14, "The Silver Fox" finished third or better in all, winning 11 times. That is the highest season winning percentage of all time. Moreover, he led more than half the laps in the races he ran and won eight poles.

Richard sees no parallel to the Petty-Pearson tug-of-war competition today. "The closest thing, if you stand back and look, is you've got Junior [Dale Earnhardt Jr.] coming along, and you already got [Jeff] Gordon. Those are the biggest names to be presented from NASCAR's standpoint.

"There's nothing even close to it. You never had it with Cale and Waltrip; it never got into anything near that big."

What is even more remarkable about the long-running Petty-Pearson rivalry is that there never was a harsh word said during it. It's almost as if Petty and Pearson were so different, and yet so fundamentally alike in their urge to race, that they regarded each other in a unique way. Richard, "The King," ran all the races, all the races. Pearson, from 1970 on, ran only the selected, paying races, descending only to Planet Petty to snatch a pole or a trophy.

"Pearson's personality and my personality, of all the people who ever ran, our personalities are probably the closest," Richard says. "I might be . . . more out-front than Pearson, but we're both laid-back. If it's raining, it's raining; don't worry about it. If the sun's shining, the sun's shining.

Pearson was always a fan favorite. In fact, fans voted in 1960 that he should get a chance at a Grand National ride. *International Motorsports Hall of Fame Archives*

Pearson, unlike Richard, was more comfortable in the shadow of the garage. Here he's contemplating the needs of his car after a practice run at the 1977 Daytona 500. *Dick Conway*

ANOTHER RIVALRY:
PETTY AND ALLISON FACE OFF

"The King" had two significant rivalries in his career—the long-lasting one he had with Pearson and the short heated one he had with Bobby Allison. The tension between the two drivers really heated up in the 1971 season, when Petty won 21 of 46 races and his fourth championship trophy and Allison won 11 races and finished fourth in points.

"Me and Allison, that was a short period of time, but it wasn't that fantastic," Richard says now in reflection. "[In] three or four races, we had the press and fans all upside-down because we was beating each other."

The feud first flared during the northern swing of the circuit at the tiny Islip, New York, track. There Petty, three or four laps ahead, tried to pass Allison, who had earlier made known his intentions to dethrone "The King."

"[Allison] didn't get out of the way or whatever," Richard says. "Chief [Maurice] and Dale [Inman] just went off. Man, they was chasing each other around when the race was over.

"So then we come back to Martinsville, do our deal, go to Wilkesboro, do our deal, then we go to Riverside. I'm trying to kind of low-key the deal in the press, while Bobby [was] keeping it going. One day after practice, Bobby came out [with] Donnie and one of their brothers. Dale and Chief were with me.

"They start out the gate, and I said, 'Hold it, we're going to talk this deal out right here. This is it. I don't want to read about any more of this in the paper.' I said to Dale and Wade and Chief, 'This goes for you and you and you. I don't want to hear nothing else about it.' I said I'd beat the snot out of the first one [who] said anything about the problems we had."

"It just stopped right there. It was over with. . . . It went away. The next thing I know, Chief and Bobby are the greatest buddies you ever seen."

Ironically, and tragically, both Richard and Bobby experienced a lot of sorrow at the end of their careers, largely as a result of the sport they had devoted their lives to. Richard's grandson, Adam, died in a wreck at New Hampshire in 2000, snuffing out the family's hopes for a fourth generation. Allison's ending was far more terrible. He suffered crippling injuries in a crash at Pocono in 1988. Then his son Clifford died in a crash at Michigan in 1992, and in 1993 son Davey died in a helicopter crash at the Talladega speedway. As a result of these tragedies, he and his wife Judy divorced. They later reconciled, in part after consoling the Petty family after Adam's death.

Allison (16) and Petty face off at Martinsville in 1975, shortly after the fiercest point of their rivalry.
Dick Conway

Pearson became Ford's flag-carrying driver in 1968 and went on to win his second championship. He won his third the following year, but finished 23rd in the points race in 1970. *Bob Tronolone*

"But when we got in a race car, we both looked at racing the same way. We don't care who leads the race, we just want to win—whatever it takes to get the job done. Then he comes up and kisses the queen and he's out of there."

Through their desire to win, the two men created a clean, genuine rivalry that still resonates decades later. Neither was ever focused on the other personally (as with Petty and Allison); it was just a matter of beating the best guy on the block. For 15 years, every time the green flag waved, each knew the other was right around the corner.

The most beautiful stat is that Petty and Pearson finished one-two an amazing 63 times over 15 years, with Pearson winning 33 of those and Petty 30. It doesn't get any closer than that, or any better.

Getting back to the 1968 season—where Petty and Pearson both ran the full schedule and both won 16 races and 12 poles—Chrysler (which backed Petty) and Ford (which backed Pearson) decided late that year that for the next season they would provide some of the most freakish cars ever allowed by NASCAR—the slope-nosed wing cars, unlike anything ever seen on the street. These cars had a high-rise spoiler and were impressive-looking vehicles—even the few that were made for the street to satisfy Big Bill France's "factory stock" requirement.

The winged cars came, over time, to be known as *birds,* regardless of marque. The name grew out of Plymouth's Superbird designation, which was matched with the Dodge Daytona and the Ford Torino. Oddly, however, the Superbird was the last out of the box,

with Dodge set to intro the model on the tracks in 1969. The Pettys, meanwhile, were contracted to the Plymouth brand.

"Here we get into politics again," Petty recalls. "I'm working for Chrysler, working for Plymouth, and Dodge comes out with a winged car. We know they're coming with a winged car, so I walk in and say, 'Where's my wing for '69?' They say, 'Man, you're winning all the races, so we're just going to leave you where you're at.'

"I'm working for Chrysler, but I drove a Plymouth. I said, 'Wait a minute, just give me a Dodge.' They said, 'No, you can't have a Dodge.' I said, 'I'll go across the street.' They said, 'Go on across the street.' "

The result was one of the most earth-shaking developments of the era. After a decade with Chrysler/Plymouth, the Pettys switched to Ford, Pearson's backer. Again, there was nothing quite like it, not even when Junior Johnson abandoned Chevrolet for Ford in 1988, or when Roger Penske turned from Ford to Dodge in 2002.

Petty and Pearson face off against fellow superstars Bobby Allison, leading in the Penske AMC Matador, and Cale Yarborough at Martinsville in 1975. In the back of the photo, observers keep track of the standings with an old, hand-operated scoreboard.
Dick Conway

Richard roots out upstart Darrell Waltrip, in his No. 17 car, late in the 1975 Martinsville spring race, where Waltrip scored his first second-place finish. By that year, Waltrip, then just 27, had begun to make an impression on the old guard. *Dick Conway*

"We just said [to Ford], 'What have you got?' " Petty explains. "They had the Torinos, which was better than the Plymouths because the Plymouths were just plain stock. The first race we ran for Ford, we went to Riverside and won the race, so that was a big plus."

"Then, about June, the president of Plymouth [Glenn White], he came down here, just showed up one day, and said, 'What will it take to get you back to Plymouth?' I said, 'Give me a wing.' So they went to work and built the Roadrunner, so in '70 we went back to them."

Richard did well in his one year with Ford, but he couldn't escape controversy that season. In fact, he faced more NASCAR tumult at the very beginning of the season. It came as a result of a new track, devised by Big Bill France and Alabama Governor George Wallace, at a little country town called Talladega.

Mission accomplished: Petty rips past the checkered flag at Martinsville. Of his 200 career victories, a record 15 came at the Virginia half-mile, an hour's drive from Level Cross. *Dick Conway*

From 1972 on, Winston took over the particulars of victory celebrations at the tracks. The trophy and, of course, Miss Winston became part of the parcel. *Dick Conway*

Coexistence? Petty fans (43) and Pearson fans (21) try to live side-by-side at the height of their rivalry in the 1970s. Yet, with the possible exception of 1974 at Daytona, the two drivers never had hard feelings between them. *Dick Conway*

Richard pulls the car in first gear as he prepares to leave the pits during practice. By the mid-1970s, a car's cockpit had seen many improvements from racing's early days, including a molded seat and fire extinguisher. *Dick Conway*

"And if elected, I promise to . . . ." Here Petty, looking almost like a political stump speaker, gestures to a surging crowd at Daytona. *Dick Conway*

"The King" established his winning ways in the 1960s, but his finest racing hours came in the 1970s, when his on-track brilliance really started to shine.
Dick Conway

The Petty-Pearson duel of the 1970s was racing's greatest rivalry. Here Richard chases down pole-winner Pearson, who is in the Woods' mighty Mercury, on the way to a World 600 win in 1977. *Dick Conway*

The duel carried cross country, with the San Gabriel Mountains of the California desert—and 50,000 eager West Coast fans—framing the action at Riverside in 1976. *Bob Tronolone*

Thanks to Petty, Pearson, and hundreds of others, Daytona in February became as much a symbol of racing as Indy in May had been for 60 years. *Dick Conway*

There was always respect, if not affection, between NASCAR's two leaders. In 1979, the Wood Brothers put Neil Bonnett in the No. 21, bumping Pearson. In a moment of great sportsmanship, Petty noticed Pearson hanging out in the pits during qualifying for the Charlotte race and went over to express his regards. *Dick Conway*

Opposite page: By 1979, Richard had been in the game for more than 20 years. He had timed thousands and thousands of laps from the comfort of the garage. *Dick Conway*

CHAPTER FIVE

TROUBLE IN TALLADEGA

"We weren't saying,
'We're not going to run your race.'
We were saying,
'Make it safe
and we'll be glad
to come down here and race.' "

The troubling, and sometimes eerie, history of the Talladega Superspeedway began almost before anybody ran the first lap. The gigantic track, just off Interstate 20 between Atlanta and Birmingham, was constructed in 1968 as a result of an agreement between Alabama Governor George Wallace, a controversial segregationist, and Bill France Sr., who were friends and political allies. What both had in mind was a track that would out-Daytona Daytona—something bigger, higher-banked, the fastest closed course in the world.

Originally christened the Alabama International Motor Speedway, Talladega, in some ways, has lived up to what its founders envisioned. It produced the first unofficial lap at 200 miles per hour (a Buddy Baker test drive in a winged Dodge in 1970), the first official 200-mile-per-hour lap (by Benny Parsons in qualifying in 1982), and NASCAR's all-time official speed record, a lap at 212.809 miles per hour by Bill Elliott in April 1987. Average speeds actually *mean* something at Talladega, where the drivers largely are flat-foot.

The track has also been the breeding ground for several ghost-friendly myths. Perhaps the most famous emerged from a report of the 1973 race, during which Bobby Isaac, contending for the lead, suddenly quit the race, saying "voices" had told him to park the car. Speculation that the track was built on sacred Creek or Cherokee ground, and hence cursed for the intrusion, has also been reported. However, no tribal group ever has stepped forward with confirming information.

More important track history, though, centers around an incipient, organized revolt by the drivers, with Richard Petty as leader, which could have changed racing in a huge way. Bill France, founder and president of NASCAR, faced down the drivers' organization, establishing once and for all—for good or otherwise—NASCAR's primacy over the competitors. There has not been a dare to the contrary since, despite occasional calls for competitor franchises. This wasn't the first attempt to organize the competitors, though. During the construction

Talladega Superspeedway was controversial even before it was built—its construction stemmed from a deal between Bill France Sr., the head of NASCAR's sanctioning body, and Alabama Governor George Wallace, a polarizing segregationist. *International Motorsports Hall of Fame Archives*

France promised that the new track, built on a former World War II air base, would become the fastest closed course in the world. It lived up to that promise. NASCAR's all-time official speed record, a lap at 212.809 miles per hour, was set there by Bill Elliott in April 1987. *International Motorsports Hall of Fame Archives*

of Charlotte Motor Speedway in 1960-1961, driver Curtis Turner, a partner in the project, sought a loan from the Teamsters Union. In exchange, the Teamsters asked that Turner help organize racers into a union called the Federation of Professional Athletes—a group apparently with an eye toward the larger goal of unionizing all professional sports. France stared that one down too, suspending Turner and cohort Tim Flock (one of NASCAR's great early champions, a contemporary and rival of Lee Petty) from competition.

The Petty-led near revolt happened after "The King" decided that the competitors—the stars—were the sport's true money-makers and thus held the power. Not surprisingly, France, conductor of races since 1936, had an entirely different view. Without the big-name stars, the promoters would have no show, Petty and other drivers argued. Yet without an organized, pursed event, the competitors would have no place to perform, France countered. The argument came to a head as the season approached—the first race set for Talladega on September 14.

By that time, Petty had organized a group of competitors (and certainly had had talks with many more) into the Professional Drivers Association (PDA), the idea being to improve the lot of drivers and crewmen with insurance, benefits, and pensions. Petty was elected president of the organization, with all the top stars participating, including Cale Yarborough, LeeRoy Yarbrough, Bobby Allison, David Pearson, Donnie Allison, and Charlie Glotzbach. The group hired noted labor attorney Lawrence Fleischer to carry its case.

"We'd just had one meeting, so we wasn't ready [for what followed]," Petty recalls. "We had this lawyer out of New York who had put the NBA deal together. I'd been up there two or three times to talk to him. We didn't have an organization. We had a name. That's about as far as it went."

As September 14 crept closer and closer, these drivers realized that, as promised, this new track in Alabama could support nearly 200-mile-per-hour speeds, but the tires available for their cars probably couldn't (they tended to distort at high speeds, which eventually caused the tires to fly off cars and break apart). Because speeds like this were not common— David Pearson hit 190-plus at Daytona earlier that year—Firestone and Goodyear did not have tires made for such velocities. The tires these companies had made to date were narrow and treaded, similar to the products made for street cars. (Remember, the *stock* concept persisted well through the 1960s, and even the Indianapolis cars used treaded tires through the 1960s.) No one had realized that by adding the tread, the tires carried too much weight to hold up to high-speed stress.

Under pressure, Firestone—at that time still privately owned—decided it could not meet the demands of the new track and abruptly pulled out.

"Goodyear wouldn't admit they couldn't make it work," Petty remembers. "Every day they were bringing a new tire, shipping 'em in overnight. They tried all kinds of compounds."

Nothing Goodyear tried that week, however, gave a satisfactory answer to the drivers, and they balked at racing at the speeds predicted, given the tire situation.

"We had complained some about some of the guardrails, some of the stuff on the track, more individually," Petty says. "Then we got down to the nitty-gritty Friday and Saturday. People who ran more than two or three laps started blowing tires off, and everybody started coming and saying, 'We've got to do something. We'll kill our crazy selves if we go out there and race.' France just said, 'Slow down.' Everywhere else, he told them to speed up.

"So we said, 'OK, that's it.' I had my crowd [the 43 team] load up. We was the first ones to load up. I told them to get up there and get in line, first in line. Then we had meetings on top of the truck—I was with Ford at the time—with all the Ford drivers. Then they got all the Ford brass. They were undecided what to do because political-wise they didn't want to be the ones who withdrew, so they said they were going to leave it up to us drivers. . . . That way France couldn't blame Ford or Chrysler. The Chrysler troupe was doing the same thing."

So the drivers basically asked for a postponement, to allow Goodyear time to develop a proper tire. "We weren't saying we're not going to run your race," Petty insists. "We were saying make it safe and we'll be glad to come down here and race.

"The drivers were just fed up with NASCAR. The deal was [that] we had something to rally behind because we'd already talked together. It really was not a per-se union strike. It was a drivers' strike, and they just happened to be all together because of the PDA."

In response, France, in one of the shrewdest moves of his career, entered a car (No. 53) with himself as driver. He boldly ran laps at his new speedway, the fastest at above 175 miles per hour, and requested entry into the driver's association.

The move didn't faze Petty and the PDA much. "The King" stuck to his stance that the track, or ultimately the tires, presented a great danger. France insisted (as the Frances always have) that if the drivers didn't want to race, NASCAR would find 40 other monkeys who would.

"We had a bunch of meetings in the garage area," Petty says. "France would get up and say his piece; then some of the drivers would get up and say their piece. I think the majority

Once Richard Petty realized that the track did support super speeds, and racing tires weren't holding up at those speeds, he started to meet with drivers in an effort to postpone the race. *International Motorsports Hall of Fame Archives*

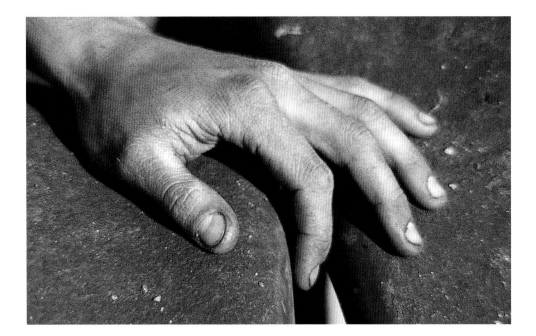

The main issue drivers had with Talladega speedway was that treaded tires did not hold up at the high-speed track. Eventually, NASCAR addressed the problem, switching to slick tires that were specially made for racing. *Dick Conway*

of 'em said [that] this is not a PDA deal, this is us, this is *me* as an individual. But on the other hand, if two or three of 'em were going to [race], the other two or three would have to follow suit because they had to keep their jobs and [didn't want] to be called chicken."

The showdown came at the end of an age of summit stand-offs—Eisenhower versus Stalin, Kennedy versus Khrushchev. And by that Saturday evening, Petty and his group—most of the top stars in NASCAR—pulled out of the Talladega event, leaving behind a scant two or three not affiliated with the PDA. France had an ace in the hole, however, with his Grand Touring division (something along the lines of the later Busch Series) also on the lot.

The GT drivers, along with a few nonjoining or defecting Grand National stars, managed to put on the first-ever race at Talladega. Richard Brickhouse won by seven seconds, at a cautious 155 miles per hour—the only race he ever won on NASCAR's big tour. Among others who participated were Bobby Isaac, Dick Brooks, Tiny Lund, Coo Coo Marlin, and Richard Childress.

Looking back over the decades, Petty is reluctant to call the driver's association a union.

"Like I told those guys to begin with, I am not a union man in any way, shape, or form," he says. "Call it an organization, that's different, but union deals, I got no time for unions because unions always take the individual out of the deal. You stand for what you can do. If you do a better job, you should be paid more than me.

"On the other hand, [a union] gives the individual a little more authority if he's got people behind him, so there's good and bad to it."

With the PDA's pullout, France was able to portray the group as running off with its tail between its legs, and he won fans over because he offered those with tickets to the 1969 Talladega event a free pass to a future race at Talladega or Daytona.

In an effort to show PDA drivers that you could drive safely at Talladega, Bill France Sr. got behind the wheel for a few laps and reached 175-plus miles-per-hour speeds. *International Motorsports Hall of Fame Archives*

Yet the PDA quietly received some long-needed concessions from the sanction, Petty says, and hence did some good for the competitors in its short life.

"I think the next month, the next week, [the sanction] called a meeting . . . at Charlotte," he recalls. "The tracks and promoters came in. That's when the [money deal] plans came in."

Petty (third from left) in an early IROC lineup. By the late 1960s and early 1970s, Richard was enough of a figure of authority to take driver concerns to the sanctioning organizations. *Dick Conway*

Petty talks things over with Pete Hamilton, Massachusetts-born ace who drove part time for the Pettys in 1970 and won the 1970 Daytona 500. *International Motorsports Hall of Fame Archives*

These plans officially regulated appearance fees, which some car owners had paid to drivers who raced all NASCAR events and some promoters had paid to top stars who made appearances at key races. After that meeting, these money deals were cemented further.

"This was NASCAR's and the tracks' reaction to what had happened at Talladega," Petty explains. "They said, 'You sign this entry blank [and] we'll give you five hundred bucks, but you promise no matter what the circumstances [are] you're going to be there.' Since '69 they've had some kind of programs, and they've got the TV program now. That all came about because of what happened in '69. Otherwise there wouldn't *be* a TV program.

Petty left his bulky Plymouth behind at the end of the 1960s. He was behind the wheel of an awesome Superbird in 1970. These were the most impressive-looking NASCAR race cars ever. Because Bill France wanted cars in the circuit to be "stock," Chrysler made a number of these vehicles for the street. *Bob Tronolone*

Yes, that's right. It's a Ford Torino wearing Petty's No. 43. The 1969 season was the Pettys' one and only with Ford, their fiercest rival through the 1960s and 1970s. *International Motorsports Hall of Fame Archives*

"We got their attention, and that's all we was trying to get done anyway. We'd go in individually and talk to NASCAR, and it would go in one ear and out the other. Once [the driver's association] happened, we didn't have to go for a while and talk to them because they went ahead and brought their end."

Petty also sees another added benefit for both sides. "When . . . we had all the trouble, that was the greatest thing that ever happened to that racetrack," he says. "Nobody knew anything about [Talladega], but that put it on the map instantly. It went off the scale because anybody who talked about Talladega talked about the problems they had down there, not who won the race or how it was won.

Richard, his body increasingly battered by 20-plus years in a brutal sport, makes the best of circumstances in preparing to meet the public after a day at the track in spring 1979. *Dick Conway*

Cale Yarborough (left) and Petty pump bicycles for a joke shot in the late 1960s. Funny thing is, this wouldn't have been a joke with a trophy on the line. *International Motorsports Hall of Fame Archives*

"It's sort of like Daytona, when Daddy and [Johnny] Beauchamp got into it. France called Beauchamp the winner, then for three or four days it was in the paper, so Daytona just jumped up there. If it had just been in Monday's paper, you'd have forgotten about it. Talladega would have been the same way, a one-day deal, a one-day wonder in the newspaper.

"It was a bad situation that both sides made work. . . . Looking back I don't see any negatives that came out of it. We got all that advertisement out of it, and we didn't hurt nobody. If we'd run a race and somebody got killed or hurt, that would have been a negative for both sides."

CHAPTER SIX

SPONSORSHIP COMES TO NASCAR

*"We got the car ready in '72
to go to [the opener at] Riverside,
a blue car like it always had been. . . .
But [Andy] Granatelli wanted a red car.
He'd always had a red car."*

Richard Petty and his team were more than winners—they were trendsetters too. Many of the present trends in racing commenced at Petty Enterprises, the most important being corporate sponsorship, which has now become the blood and breath of racing in the NASCAR world.

Before 1970, owners and drivers relied pretty much on their own resources and, in the case of the major operations, on factory support. Then as 1970 approached, and the muscle car era was winding down, government regulations seemed to dictate fuel economy and safety over raw power. Some in Detroit also sensed the coming petroleum crisis in the Middle East, which would have crippling effects on America (and racing) in 1973 and 1974 as the OPEC cartel decided to wield its power.

These factors pushed the auto factories to suddenly pull out of racing in 1970 and 1971, leaving the sport high and dry of much of its equipment and financial backing. The move put Holman-Moody out of business, although Ford transferred support under the table to the Wood Brothers and Bud Moore, who via drag racing helped develop the Ford 351. In fact, for a decade, just about everything from Detroit was under the table, and many competitors had to resort to pure stock bodies and junkyard Chevy 350s. The Pettys, however, had contracts with Chrysler, which were honored regardless of the pullout, so no one was really suffering in Level Cross.

Then came the two developments that really changed the course of NASCAR history. First, R. J. Reynolds Tobacco, shut out of most advertising outlets because of new regulations, found a connection with Bill France Sr. via Junior Johnson and Ralph Seagraves. The tobacco company, based in Winston-Salem, North Carolina, had longtime and favorable connections with racing and its people, and the step to series sponsorship was natural and very timely. What R. J. Reynolds (RJR) brought to NASCAR was its marketing savvy and power, which dated back to the turn of the century. The company had millions of marketing dollars bound up now that tobacco ads were banned from the airwaves, and buying into NASCAR was a bargain at a reported $2 million for the first season.

With sponsorship, RJR lifted NASCAR out of the dust and grease of its past, dictating that it would not sponsor events of less than 250 miles—thus bringing reduction of the

Yes, other drivers did have sponsors in 1971 when STP decided to back the Petty car. But no sponsor had funded an entire racing season, which is what STP did when Richard's car became a mix of Petty blue and STP red. Here is an early look at the new No. 43 car with Walter Ballard's Clyde Lynn–sponsored car in front of it. *Dick Conway*

The Pettys knew how to keep marketing their own brand, Petty Enterprises. They always touted their "Level Cross" products on the track. *Dick Conway*

The No. 43 car sporting the badge of its
sponsor at Riverside in 1974 and 1976.
Bob Tronolone

NASCAR schedule to 30 or so races. It set up a points structure and championship fund.
It also took over sponsorship of the spring Talladega race, making it immediately one
of the biggest and best. And then there was the paint: Winston's red-and-white paint,
not to mention new scoreboards and signage, helped upgrade dilapidated tracks such
as Richmond, Nashville, Riverside, and North Wilkesboro, and gave the circuit a more
uniform and professional look.

A more direct benefit to the Pettys came when STP decided it wanted to be a part of
NASCAR racing. STP, an oil-additive producer based in Chicago, had steered into Indy
cars in 1964, first with the Unsers, then with Parnelli Jones, and then with Art Pollard. STP
was not a big company (although it later went through two or three acquisitions by larger
companies), but in this era of racing it could afford to back a race car. It first sponsored
the Ray Nichels Plymouth team and driver Fred Lorenzen in 1971. Later with Andy
Granatelli serving as its racing program leader, the company decided it wanted to partner
with "The King" of stock car racing.

"The factories basically got out in '70," Petty recalls. "Everybody already had their stuff, and we had an extended contract with Chrysler. [Then] . . . in the middle of '71, the Chrysler deal was running out. At that time, no major sponsors were involved in racing."

As a result, Petty Enterprises hooked up with Granatelli, first discussing a sponsorship in the fall of 1971. "We went to Texas for the last race in '71, and Granatelli showed up and we talked. We never really came to a conclusion. It was still back and forth on the phone, and it didn't look like anything was going to happen," Richard recalls.

Later on in the negotiations, the color blue became a sticking point. The famous "Petty Blue" had become Richard's trademark through the 1960s; it had become a racing standard—the medium-blue No. 43 *was* Richard Petty, everywhere in the United States and around the world. The color was almost a battle flag in the presponsorship days.

"We got the car ready in '72 to go to [the opener at] Riverside, a blue car like it always had been. Me and Dale [Inman] and Maurice went to Chicago to talk to Granatelli. We talked and

Here the red's back as Richard races at speed on the Richmond track early in the 1974 season. *Dick Conway*

talked. The money deal come across, [and] everything was fine. But Granatelli wanted a red car. He'd always had a red car. I said, 'We've always had a blue car, damn it, and I don't care how much money you've got.' We were hard-headed people, and he was hard-headed. Their PR guy said, 'OK, we'll try to work this thing out. You spend the night.' "

The next morning the group agreed to make the car half blue, half red, and a couple of days later, in 1972, the deal was announced at the Riverside, California, road course.

"They had a big press conference, and [Granatelli] gets up and says, 'We're going Cup racing,' " Richard says. "He had his signs out, and at exactly ten o'clock Ralph Salvino walks over and puts a decal on the side of the car. He had to coordinate that. He had the press there. That became the first national sponsorship. . . . That was the beginning."

Petty may be just a little too bold in saying so, as many other companies had put their logos on NASCAR race cars before, going as far back as the 1950s. Remember Wynn's and Perfect Circle? Some of those deals were for cash, others for product, but none of them could finance an entire season. The STP deal, for a reported $200,000, was huge, at least equaling a factory job.

With years now gone by, many fans have forgotten that the Pettys existed before STP. The STP logo and the No. 43 quickly became linked in everyone's minds in the 1970s and by the end of the decade, most people could not imagine Richard Petty without the STP logo, or vice versa.

Around the same time as the STP deal, other companies lined up for full sponsorship deals. Purolator, maker of filters and other automotive products, hunted up the Wood Brothers. Coca-Cola made a deal with Junior Johnson. Breweries (Carling and Budweiser), soft drink makers (Pepsi and Mountain Dew), and even companies that made suntan lotions and pantyhose flocked to get a piece of the action.

"The game just went from there," Petty says with wonder. "You've got everything now."

The Pettys also accelerated the trend toward multi-car teams during this period. They had fielded companion cars in the early 1960s, with Jim Paschal as their first number two driver, and as the 1970s began, they, for various reasons, enlisted young chargers such as Buddy Baker and Pete Hamilton, a pleasant, dashing Yankee from Massachusetts. Hamilton won three of his 15 starts in the Petty Plymouths in 1970, including, remarkably, the Daytona 500.

The opportunity with Baker developed from the remains of the Chrysler factory deal. "Buddy'd been driving for Cotton [Owens]," Richard notes. "Cotton didn't have a deal for '70, so we took Buddy up here. Chrysler wanted to run a Plymouth and a Dodge, so we brought Buddy up here because we were the factory people at the time. Pete went to Cotton. I think they had a Plymouth, and they had a sponsor for a few races. Buddy came up here and won two or three races for us that year [actually, one each year in 1971 and 1972], so we ran two cars off and on."

That arrangement ended in 1972, as NASCAR stabilized around the 30-race schedule. The fabulous and freakish 1960s decade had officially passed by then, and NASCAR and its teams had started to buckle down and get back to old-fashioned racing.

Petty's Dodge shows a battle scar on the driver door. The rub mark wiped out the original NASCAR trademark, but the original Winston racing logo above it is intact. *Dick Conway*

A man of many hats, Richard turns down the brim of his so-called "mountain" hat while waiting for the start of a race in 1974. *Dick Conway*

Yes, that's Richard in casual "work" attire—cowboy boots, sleeves rolled, STP hat—looking on as crewmen work on the No. 43 Dodge. *Dick Conway*

Without factory support, teams had to work out the bugs in the plain and plentiful old small-block engines (the Chevrolet 350 and Ford 351), which had been the backbone of stock car racing since 1955. The mutations of the 1960s—big-blocks, hemis, and winged Torinos—were products of a fantastic era that was now over.

"What they tried to do then, NASCAR said, [was] too much," Petty explains. "[The sport] got away from them, so they brought it back stock. The technology then was what Junior [Johnson] could come up with, what the Wood boys could come up with, and what the Pettys could come up with in their backyard. So we took what we learned from [the factories] and made it a little bit better, and just escalated it along a little bit at a time.

"The cars were better next year than they were the year before. Aerodynamically they were better. We weren't running wind tunnels. We didn't know what a wind tunnel was except for airplanes. They looked like stock cars—had chrome, had bumpers. So it went along pretty good with just the ingenuity of a few people."

Petty wheels his damaged Dodge through the turns at Riverside in the January 1975 race. Petty nevertheless finished seventh, several laps behind winner Bobby Allison. *Bob Tronolone*

This is one of the later-model Dodges that Petty drove as the 1970s wound down and Chrysler's support diminished. The Pettys would switch to General Motors cars by the end of the decade. *Bob Tronolone*

Now that the sport's waters were somewhat settled, Big Bill, now 61, decided in 1972 to step aside, giving control of the organization to his son, William C. France, better known as Bill Jr., or Billy. Billy, just 38, was seen as a callow kid, a shadow of his father, but he guided the ship steadily, with an eye for business yet without his father's bluster and showmanship.

In some ways, what followed was NASCAR's golden age. The cars were cheap, sponsorship was optional, and the number of big-dollar teams was low—the Pettys, the Woods, Junior Johnson. If you had a decent race car and could afford the travel, you could make racing pay. Drivers making a name for themselves included established stars such as Cale Yarborough, 1970 NASCAR champion Bobby Isaac, the Allison brothers, and emerging stars such as Benny Parsons and Darrell Waltrip.

Petty added to his royal kingdom during this era with his fourth championship in 1972. It was the year he turned 34 and the first year the title was a Winston Cup–branded honor. He and his team also spent time that year refining the dependable 1972 Dodge Charger, the model that became their template for most of the decade and is still most identified with Petty Blue.

This is a view of remote Rockingham, in the North Carolina Sandhills, with Petty following Cale Yarborough around Bruce Hill (47) and Dave Marcis (71). Despite the lack of corporate display, the event attracted the likes of Roger Penske and A. J. Foyt. *Dick Conway*

Even though Richard won his fourth Daytona 500 in 1973, it wasn't his year. He failed to finish in 10 of 28 starts, dropping him to fifth in the final standings. Instead, newcomer Parsons was the golden boy that year, running in contention all season—only doing so in the Rockingham race after other teams contributed parts and labor to keep him in.

Petty won his fifth Daytona 500, and fifth championship, in 1974, nearly running away with the points title with 13 wins. Yarborough finished second, with Pearson—who had another superlative season, winning 11 times in 19 starts—finishing third.

In 1975 at Talladega, tragedy struck Petty Enterprises when Randy Owens—brother of Richard's wife Lynda and a dependable, longtime crewman—was killed by an exploding water tank in the pits. Richard equated that moment with his drag racing disaster in 1965 and with the death of Adam in 2000. "Those were the lowest points [of my career]," he says.

Yet, Petty—just like he had in 1965 and would again in 2000—picked up the pieces and went on, on to greater success in the last half of the decade.

Opposite page: The field is lined up for the start on the backstretch at Martinsville before the spring race in 1975. Benny Parsons' No. 72 is inside-front, on the pole. Petty, outside-front, won the race. *Dick Conway*

The front valence, an aero device, began to develop in the mid-1970s, and the Pettys and STP quickly adapted it as advertising space, displaying STP's "The Racer's Edge" slogan. *Dick Conway*

Petty team crewmen hung their jackets on a rack before going to work in the garage at Daytona. Even without the men, the colors symbolized the Pettys, STP, and racing itself. *Dick Conway*

Opposite page: The STP flag waves high, along with the Confederate flag as Petty, Bobby Allison, Neil Bonnett, and Cale Yarborough battle on the track at Charlotte. *Dick Conway*

CHAPTER SEVEN

TWO FANTASTIC FINISHES

═

"We looked down the back stretch
and didn't see nothing,
but they [the leaders] was like twenty seconds ahead,
half a lap ahead,
and they done crashed."

Two moments in the 1970s—both involving Richard Petty, and both at Daytona, NASCAR's greatest stage—stand out in the history of racing—*all* forms of racing history. The first was wild finish of the Daytona 500 in 1976, with Petty and Pearson bumping and crashing to the finish line—the climax of racing's greatest rivalry. The second was the ending of 1979 500, where Petty won, but a near brawl was the defining highlight in NASCAR's first live television coverage of an entire 500-mile race.

It's almost a shame the 1976 race wasn't the first one CBS broadcasted in its entirety. In this race, the Petty/Pearson, Dodge/Mercury rivalry hits its ultimate peak, with an unscripted ending beyond imagination. On the last of the 200 laps, Petty and Pearson were all alone in front, with Richard leading through the first and second turns. Pearson, sizing up his last chance, made his move to the inside into Turn 3, but he couldn't hold his car down and pushed high, leaving an opening inside for Petty. As the crowd of 80,000 rose to its feet with a roar, Petty edged ahead off the final turn.

Then Petty, in attempting to block Pearson, made a mistake. As he let his car drift toward the high side, the right-rear of his Dodge clipped the nose of Pearson's Mercury, and hell broke loose, with both cars hitting the outside wall and spinning toward the inside. Petty's engine stopped in the tri-oval grass, whereas Pearson had to presence to clutch his engine, leaving it running. As Petty desperately cranked his machine, Pearson's car got nipped by the trailing car of Joe Frasson, turning the Mercury toward the finish line.

With 300 yards to go and his car in tatters, Pearson crept to the finish line at 20 miles per hour, capturing his first and only Daytona 500 victory, while Petty's crew rushed to the grass and tried to push him home.

The crowd went nuts. The two greatest racers of the decade had put on the greatest show of the decade.

It was a characteristic glimpse of the two men's career-long duel that not a harsh word was spoken after this showdown. "It was just a racing deal, and Pearson would have done the same thing," Richard recalls. "The crews didn't know that, so they were upset. I sat my people down and told them Pearson hadn't done anything wrong, that he just happened to be there when I moved. We didn't have spotters back then, so I didn't know I wasn't clear."

Richard now says this about the 1976 race's impact on his legacy: "I tell people there's three things I'm known for about Daytona: the '88 wreck, everybody knows about that; the '76 race; and third, winning some races. Those two races outshone my winning."

And as for his unprecedented seven Daytona wins, Richard sees them this way: "Probably four of 'em I really just outrun everybody and I should have won. There's two or three of 'em that if somebody hadn't had bad luck, like '79, I wouldn't have won. But then there's three or four others if I hadn't had bad luck I would have won. So it evens itself up.

"Between me and him [Pearson], we was winning everything, know what I mean? Here's the two top dogs. You had the two biggest names racing each other to something like that. It wasn't like you had a sixteenth-place man you never heard tell of. It wouldn't have been so dramatic then."

In the 1976–1977 season—while Cale Yarborough began emerging as a genuine force under the tutelage of Junior Johnson—the Chrysler racing effort, which had been officially abandoned by the company but still was run under the table, began to deteriorate. Petty won just three races in 1976, his lowest number since 1961, and finished second to Yarborough in the standings. The next year, Petty won five times and again finished second to Yarborough.

Then, in 1978, Chrysler/Dodge introduced its new, boxy Magnum model, which just never got off the ground. By the time of the summer race at Daytona that season, only four drivers were running Dodges, and of those only Petty was remotely competitive. But he

Richard lets the rough side drag off-course through the dirt at Riverside in 1977. During this January race, Petty rallied to third place, finishing a lap behind winner David Pearson. *Bob Tronolone*

wasn't even that competitive—for the first time since 1959, "The King" failed to win a single race. He managed to place second just three times: at North Wilkesboro in the spring and at Martinsville and Atlanta in the fall.

Petty, by this time, had been hard at it for 20 years, gritty and exhausting campaigns that totaled 774 races and 185 victories. Talk began to circulate that "The King," now 41, was looking at the down side of the winning hill. The rumors escalated when Pearson, Petty's fierce rival for more than a decade, started considering retirement because he wasn't winning much either.

At one point, the duo actually joked about their recent misfortunes. "My cars are not as good as they used to be," Pearson told reporters. "Richard? To tell you the truth, Richard is just over the hill."

Then Pearson continued, with a laugh: "No, I can understand Richard's problem. I haven't run good since we had to change body styles with the Mercury two years ago. Now Richard is going through the same thing with the new Dodge."

In fact, Maurice and Dale Inman had kept the 1972-type Dodge Charger alive and kicking for six years, until the model was discontinued after NASCAR required (under its old "stock" mandates) the change to the newer Dodge.

The displacement of an engine became part of a stock car's hood display during the 1970s. In the early 1970s, NASCAR made the transition from big-block to small-block engines, yet the Pettys preferred the big 426 Hemi at most tracks. *Dick Conway*

Petty realized the true source of his woes in the April race at Bristol. After crashing out early, he relieved fatigued driver Lennie Pond, driving Harry Ranier's Chevrolet, and brought it home fifth. The Pettys then accelerated their plans to switch to the bow-tie make. Richard made his first start in a Chevrolet that summer at Michigan, thus ending a fabulous era with Chrysler, Plymouth, and Dodge. But he took a beating in that debut. One of his car's tires blew late in the race, pitching him into the wall. Several of his ribs cracked upon impact.

Earlier that year, Petty had undergone stomach surgery to relieve his ulcer problems. He had already put the surgery off for three years and the pain was beginning to take a toll on him. But surgery also changed him—from the robust young man who set all the

On a Friday afternoon at Richmond, with only a small crowd in the stands, Petty slides into the car for qualifying. In the background, the flagman waves another car past the clock. *Dick Conway*

records and attracted all the fans, to the rail-thin fellow with a big belt buckle and plumed cowboy hat. His demanding life and health problems were starting to age him. Yet, from late-1971 on, Richard never missed a race, despite occasional serious pains and increasing responsibilities as leader of a growing sport.

Hence 1979 was pivotal, and all the more triumphant, given that Petty had lost three championships in a row, had been blanked in the wins column the season before, and had come to be seen as someone who should . . . well . . . should get out before things got worse. Then came the race that is considered the most epochal battle in NASCAR's first 50 years—the 1979 Daytona 500.

Baseball and football were long-established network television sports by then. Yet for the most part, NASCAR's large-audience exposure had been through condensed replays on *Wide World of Sports* and other network digest programs. So anticipation was high when NASCAR made a deal with CBS for live start-to-finish coverage of the 1979 Daytona 500.

Richard talks with local reporter Randy Hallman at Richmond in 1975. The red jacket is a monogrammed one with his initials, "RLP," on the breast pocket. *Dick Conway*

Crew chief Dale Inman, at the driver's door, moves the No. 43 car toward the qualifying line. Behind Inman at the rear fender is Maurice Petty, who has answered to the nickname "Chief" all his life. *Dick Conway*

Petty, flanked by adoring trophy queens, seems unaffected in victory lane after winning at Riverside in summer 1977, one of five wins for "The King" that season.
Bob Tronolone

Early in the race, Darrell Waltrip, A. J. Foyt, and Petty tore away from the crowd. The ending was a blockbuster, a bomb blast that still resonates decades later.

On the last lap, Donnie Allison led the race, with Yarborough second, Petty third, and Waltrip fourth. Off Turn 2, Yarborough darted to the inside of Allison. Allison blocked, and the two cars bounced off each other twice before spinning to the inside in Turn 3. The two men climbed out of their cars and approached each other and began a fight for the ages. Petty and Waltrip meanwhile sailed by to the finish line. It was Petty's sixth Daytona 500 victory, far and away the record.

As the cameras focused on the fracas in Turn 3, Donnie's brother Bobby, circling the last lap, came to a stop to help, climbing out and joining in the tangle. CBS had it all live on camera. Millions on the East Coast saw every moment as they were tuned in, stuck at home in the midst of a winter storm.

What they saw on CBS was NASCAR at its most contentious and dramatic moment—the single event that put this sport in the media's crosshairs and in the public's minds.

"The race stopped when they stopped," Petty recalls. "I don't know who was third or fourth. We came off the second corner and the caution lights went on. Foyt just automatically lifted, then he realized what was going on—but he was out of the game. Me and Darell, we didn't know what the caution was, didn't have radios, so we didn't have a clue whether the caution was behind us.

"We looked down the back stretch and didn't see nothing, but they [the leaders] was like twenty seconds ahead, half a lap ahead, and they done *crashed*. They was down on the infield. So we went around, and Darrell was trying to get by, and there's two cars down there—'Damn, that's the leaders,' I thought.

"So anyhow, we come back and I beat him to the deal and won the race."

Also lost in the hubbub, in many ways, was the rejuvenation of Richard and Petty Enterprises, for the 1979 season. He only won five races and a pole that year, but he finished in the top 10 in 27 of 31 events. He also earned a career high $561,934, the highest season total to date by any driver, augmented by the ever-increasing Winston points fund.

What may have been most impressive, though, was the way "The King" triumphed in one of the closest and most bitter points races of all time in 1979. Going into the Dover race, sixth from the end, Petty trailed young hot rod Waltrip—now nearing the top of his game with DiGard—by 187 points. He won at Dover, with Waltrip placing 29th, and cut the cap in half. He halved the margin again with a second-place finish the next week at Martinsville, his home track.

Petty finally took the lead three races from the finish with a victory at Rockingham. Waltrip's finish put him just eight points behind. At Atlanta, the next-to-last event, Waltrip finished fifth and Petty sixth, so Waltrip recaptured the lead by two.

The finale at Ontario, California, would determine the winner. Petty struggled to fifth place, with Waltrip eighth, and won the championship by 11 points, the closest margin until 1992. More importantly though, "The King" had proven to the world that he was still up for a fight after all.

STP gear was plentiful in 1975, so plentiful in fact that up-and-coming youngster Darrell Waltrip, soon to be one of Petty's fiercest rivals, wore one of Richard's caps during an interview at Martinsville. *Dick Conway*

Sure, you can pick out Richard, Buddy Baker, and Cale Yarborough here, but can you spot Buddy Arrington, Lennie Pond, Richard Childress, J. D. McDuffie, or Chuck Bown? *Dick Conway*

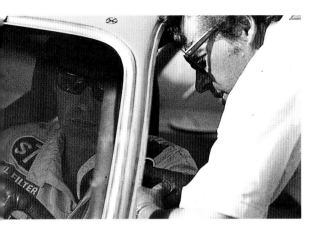

Crew chief Dale Inman talks over the car's handling with Richard during a practice session at Martinsville. Inman, a keen strategist, was also a master of car setup. *Dick Conway*

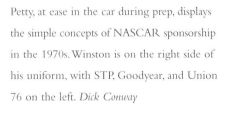

Petty, at ease in the car during prep, displays the simple concepts of NASCAR sponsorship in the 1970s. Winston is on the right side of his uniform, with STP, Goodyear, and Union 76 on the left. *Dick Conway*

The parade lap at magnificent Ontario (California) Speedway in fall 1977, the last race of the season. Petty, the pole-winner, finished second. Neil Bonnett, outside-front at the start, was the winner. *Bob Tronolone*

Dale Inman shares a joke with Lennie Pond in 1975. Pond—rookie of the year in 1973, beating out Darrell Waltrip—was a promising contender through the 1970s. *Dick Conway*

Petty only sported a beard for a short time in 1976, here looking more like a lion in a cage than a driver in a car. *Dick Conway*

Petty (inside) challenges Darrell Waltrip (outside) early at Charlotte in 1976. *Dick Conway*

Petty digs for a gear through Turn 8 at Riverside. Note the precise and flowing contours of the Dodge and the increasing emphasis on increasing air intake by altering the design of the grille. Also note the utterly simple rear-view mirror. *Bob Tronolone*

Petty, now driving a Chevy Monte Carlo, wheels through the fourth turn at Ontario in November 1979. Petty came to Ontario needing to beat Darrell Waltrip by three or four places in order to clinch his record seventh championship. Richard finished fifth to Waltrip's eighth and won the title by 11 points, the closest gap in history at the time. *Bob Tronolone*

Richard rubs his way past Dick Brooks at Martinsville in 1975, with Cale Yarborough (11) and Bobby Allison (16) dead ahead. *Dick Conway*

Enterprising fans watch the Richmond race for free from trees just outside the track, which in the late 1970s still had a board fence and steel rails. They are getting quite a treat as "The King" pursues Buddy Baker (28) and Cale Yarborough (11). *Dick Conway*

Here's the best view in the house, though. This is the start of the Richmond race in September 1977 as seen from the shotgun side of the pace car, which just has been pulled to pit road. Benny Parsons leads, followed by Neil Bonnett (5) and Bobby Allison (12).

Dominating: Petty puts another lap on
Buddy Baker at Rockingham in March
1976. Richard led 362 of the 492 laps and
won by more than two laps over Darrell
Waltrip. Baker finished fourth. *Dick Conway*

Petty hangs it out through the gravel and berm at Riverside in January 1977. In his prime, Richard was an excellent road-race performer, with five wins and four poles at the California course. *Bob Tronolone*

"The King" guides a modified Camaro at Riverside during an International Race of Champions round in 1977. Indy champ Gordon Johncock chases him. Others in the race included road racers Al Holbert and Jody Sheckter and Indy heroes Bobby Unser, Al Unser, Johnny Rutherford, and A. J. Foyt. *Bob Tronolone*

Compare Petty's 1978 Dodge with the cars that followed. Aerodynamics? Minimal. Spoiler? Don't see it. Yet, many argue that the racing was better then than it is now.

Dick Conway

Petty leads Waltrip and Pearson past the flag stand in the 1978 Daytona 500 race, just before the wreck that destroyed the hopes of the three front-runners. *Dick Conway*

Crewmen rush to Petty's car after the big wreck during the 1978 Daytona 500. Richard walks away from the car, holding his sore shoulder. *Dick Conway*

It didn't take an engineer to prep a car in the 1970s. A roll of tape, a set of SAE sockets, a pair of Vise-Grips, a couple sets of spark plugs, and a bag of shop rags put you in the game. *Dick Conway*

CHAPTER EIGHT

KYLE:

THE NEXT GENERATION

—

"Even as a kid,
[Kyle] was always an individual. . . .
He was his own man.
He's still that way,
and far as I'm concerned,
I'm really glad he's that way."

Kyle Petty, the oldest of Richard Petty's four children and his only son, had to wait until he was 18 and had graduated from high school to start driving a race car—that was the family rule.

Before that, he spent his time like most teens do—playing football, baseball, and basketball for his high school team, the Randleman High School Tigers. He even was a good enough athlete that he was recruited by several university programs.

"We didn't grow up in an environment like kids do today, computers at school, this and that. We didn't have a lot of options," Kyle says. "I went to a school where the guys played every sport because if everybody didn't play, they didn't have enough to have a team."

He also tried to live a normal life, even though he knew his family was different, almost exalted.

"We live in rural North Carolina where most everybody has farms," Kyle says. "So we lived here, Uncle Maurice lived across the road, and the next-closest neighbor was about a mile down this way—this road was dirt until '72.

"We got up in the morning, went to the end of the driveway, caught a bus, went to school, came home in the afternoon, and dropped our stuff off. Then I came to the race shop for three or four hours."

Yes, that's where Kyle's life was different from his friends'.

"We had race cars," he says with a smile. "You're hanging out at a place where they're building cars, and that just didn't happen everywhere. Most people didn't build cars. But here they were working on engines, working on cars, always different people coming by. They built drag cars for Sox and Martin, Roy Hill—guys like that. Uncle Maurice built engines for people who had boats, street cars, always a mix of people.

"So you come by and they let you sweep. Then they teach you how to weld. Then they let you weld a piece that didn't really make any difference, but they put it on the car. Then I ended up working for Dale [Inman] and Wade and that crowd. They let you sandblast stuff, paint it, and Magnaflux it. They made me kind of work in each place, not be an expert at anything but learn a little about everything. From the time I was in third grade on, I spent almost all my time over here with this crowd. As I got older, I started doing more and more."

When Kyle started driving, everyone started to anticipate the day he would accompany and/or succeed his father in the family car, in the family business.

His first step toward that came in the winter of 1979, when he made his stock car racing debut at Daytona of all places, driving a Petty-prepared car in the ARCA preliminary. ARCA was, and is, a poor man's parallel universe to NASCAR. The cars are nearly identical, as are the race formats, and ARCA also runs at the many of the same tracks, and during the same weekends, as Cup events do.

Kyle, 18, thrown cold into the Daytona shark pond, had a superior car and won his very first race start easily. The effect was brilliant, comparable to the public starburst surrounding Dale Earnhardt Jr.'s first NASCAR entries in 1997 and 1998. The Pettys then pulled up their belts and entered Kyle at the May Talladega race in a No. 42 Dodge.

That was his first race in what then was called Winston Cup. He finished ninth. In the eyes of many, the pedigree had carried on to the third generation.

Kyle made four more entries in 1979, all at big tracks, and he ran credibly. The Pettys then stepped it up a gear in 1980. Kyle ran 15 races in Petty Chevrolets under STP/Petty colors (identical to Richard's paint) and scored a best of seventh place. The ball was rolling, but Richard, always the realist, knew it could not roll far.

Young Kyle, with open-face helmet and goggles askance, gets a grip on the wheel prior to qualifying for a race in 1980. *Dick Conway*

Some effort was made to match Kyle's look with his father's when the younger Petty started his career. It would take more than a hat, however, to make the two men comparable. *Dick Conway*

"We had one sponsor and two race cars—not enough money," he says. "We were trying to get Kyle started like we tried to get Adam started [in the late 1990s], so we were draining resources away from my car basically to Kyle's car. We didn't have enough money to do the things we needed to do, so we were short-changing both sides.

"We didn't do it right, OK? Looking back on it, I was so engrossed in my career that [getting Kyle racing] was sort of a sideline deal instead of . . . the way it should have been done—an equal deal [where] he's the next guy and you've got to take this deal and put it into him."

Kyle remembers it much the same way. "Our biggest problem was [that] Richard Petty was extremely loyal, if you want to call that a problem," he says. "We had STP, and STP was enough for one car, not enough for two cars. In hindsight, we probably shouldn't have done it, but for all STP had meant for our family and to him especially, it was a big deal. So we ran four or five races in '79, then I ran fifteen races in '80 and started running full time in '81. I was in an STP car in '81."

The 1981 season started strong at Petty Enterprises. Richard opened the year with one of his finest triumphs, winning the 1981 Daytona 500. That was his seventh, and last, Daytona 500 win and the 193rd win of his career.

Petty had tested a Dodge before the season, raising excitement of a possible return to the family marque. The car was too slow, however, and the team instead chose the Buick.

In addition, NASCAR had mandated a change in wheelbase, reducing from 115 inches to 110, hence confusing matters further that season.

Bobby Allison, driving for Harry Ranier, arrived at Daytona with a Pontiac, having tested in the off-season out of sight at Talladega. The car was superior, with Allison winning his qualifying heat and drawing raves as the favorite for the 500. In the race, he led 117 of the 200 laps. Yet Petty and crew, led as always by Dale Inman, were closely watching tire wear throughout the race, so when drivers made their final pit stops with 25 laps to go and Allison and Buddy Baker pitted for tires and fuel, Petty only gassed up and emerged from the pits with a 10-second lead. Despite a furious charge by Allison, Petty kept his lead, winning by better than three seconds.

"We saw we could handle as good as everyone else under the circumstances, but no one was faster than Bobby down the straights," Petty said at the time. "So it was the crew that delivered this win. I leave the strategy to them. I'm too busy out there racing.

"Dale's got full authority, and when he told me we weren't using up the tires, I radioed back that I would do whatever he thought was right. So when it came time to play follow-the-leader down pit road, we didn't follow. It was Dale's call."

Petty continued to perform well in the following races, holding the points lead through the fourth race at Rockingham. But then the strains on Petty Enterprises started to show. From Atlanta in March through Charlotte in May, Richard failed to finish seven of nine races—four due to mechanical failures. Overall, he recorded 13 DNFs that season, winning three times and finishing eighth in points, well behind emergent champion Darrell Waltrip.

Also, that season was Kyle's first full season in Cup races, but the promise shown in 1979 had been left at just that—*promise.* Kyle's year, like his father's, was marginal (at least by Petty standards), with Kyle showing DNFs in an astonishing 18 of 31 races; 16 of those failures were mechanical—an indication that Kyle wasn't getting the best of the best. His best finish was fifth at Charlotte.

Moreover, Dale Inman, part of the group since the 1950s and crew chief since the late 1960s, abruptly quit in mid-1981, going to work elsewhere. "I think in his mind he thought he couldn't do some of the things he wanted to do because it was me and Chief [Maurice] and Daddy, so he had three boss men," Richard explains. "One day, I guess he just woke up and said, 'I don't need this.'"

All of these factors put serious dents in the Petty Enterprises armor. The group could no longer be considered the dominant force it had been during the prior two decades.

Through the fall and winter, the group tried to collect its wits and reorganize the team, with young Steve Hmiel taking charge of the shop and pits. More importantly, Petty Enterprises ended its longtime exclusive relationship with STP by agreeing to partial sponsorship on Kyle's cars from UNO, a Mattel card game (that, incidentally, commenced a longer-term relationship between the Pettys and Mattel).

Things did not improve in 1982, however. Richard went winless for the first time since 1978—only the second time in his career—and although he improved to fifth in points, he

Kyle eased into NASCAR with 15 starts in 1980, twice at the Martinsville home ground. The No. 42 had been run by others, notably Marty Robbins, since the retirement of Lee Petty in the early 1960s. Kyle brought it back to life. *Dick Conway*

again suffered through 13 DNFs. Kyle's year was worse, with 17 failures, all but one of them mechanical. Realizing they needed a separate sponsor for Kyle, the Pettys accepted an opportunity in 1983 to banner Kyle's cars in the colors of 7-Eleven. From that point, though, father and son began to follow divergent paths.

Kyle always was a free spirit. Raised amid fame and opportunity, and with the difficult role as son of a legend, he sought his own goals, leading some to wonder whether he took racing seriously. He let his hair grow, wore earrings, and made a fairly dedicated foray into

Kyle's clean and trim No. 42 makes a pit stop at Martinsville in 1980. His entries required extra men for the prep and pit crews, with not a lot more money from STP.

Dick Conway

the Nashville music scene, taking part in a couple of albums. He had some musical ability and even went far enough with it to secure an agent.

"He was wanting to do his own thing, wanting to prove his own thing," Richard says, glancing over to his son. "He's still so independent."

"Kyle Petty is not Richard Petty," "The King" adds with understanding in his voice. "I don't talk like him, I don't walk like him. I'm an individual. I was fortunate enough when I came along behind Lee Petty [that] there wasn't that press, there wasn't that pressure. They never compared me. I never read anything anywhere where anybody ever compared Richard Petty against Lee Petty, and Lee Petty was better.

"Kyle comes along and wins at Daytona, and he's compared already—*the next Richard Petty*—and the press got him started in that direction. But even as a kid, he was always an individual. If everybody had short hair, he had long hair. If everybody had long hair, he came

February in Richmond: After the sunshine at Daytona, the trip north to Virginia always brings out everyone's hats and coats. Here a bundled up Richard works out race details with Dale Inman in the Richmond pits in 1980. *Dick Conway*

and got a crew cut. He was his own man. He's still that way, and far as I'm concerned, I'm really glad he's that way."

Kyle's eventual departure from Petty Enterprises came in part out of that spirit, but also because even with the 7-Eleven deal, both Pettys were trying to run their cars on minimal resources. "We signed up with 7-Eleven, and even with that, we were trying to run two teams on enough money to run one-and-a-half teams," Kyle says. "We had the established star in Richard Petty, and we had an unknown quantity here, so you couldn't get the money. [Two cars] didn't equate like it does now, so it got to a point where it would be better for one of us to leave."

In the first 20 years of Richard's career, the pit stop constantly became more and more choreographed. Here Richard's brother Maurice mans the air hose. *Dick Conway*

Even into the late 1970s, the Pettys continued to field extra cars for sharp drivers. Joe Millikan (04), who challenged Dale Earnhardt for rookie of the year in 1979, chases all-time great Ray Hendrick in the 1978 Daytona NASCAR Sportsmen 300 race. Joe was a neighbor of the Pettys in Randleman, North Carolina. *Dick Conway*

Adding to the behind-the-scenes tension was an unfathomable twist in the Petty story: Richard Petty was caught cheating at Charlotte in late 1983. He, according to officials, had incorrect tires (fact) on his car and an oversized engine (still somewhat questionable).

Petty had won that race, his 198th victory and third of the season, but was told by crew chief Larry Pollard afterward that the crew had put left-side tires on the right side of the car during the final pit stop, after which Richard blasted toward the checkered flag. It is against NASCAR regulations to mismount tires; left-side tires generally are softer, and the softer rubber on the right made a difference in the short run.

Moreover, NASCAR inspectors also cubed Petty's engine at about 370 ci, well over the 358-ci limit. At least that's the story—no one knows for sure what the real size was. NASCAR then debated for hours as to how to handle penalizing its greatest star. Long after dark, NASCAR announced that victory number 198 would stand, but that Petty would be penalized $35,000 and 104 championship points. That was the largest such penalty in NASCAR history at the time.

"The King" caught cheating—the impact was enormous. "It's like accusing God of sinning," a sorrowful fan told a reporter. Others wondered if Richard Petty, a man of legendary integrity, would accept a winning trophy under such conditions. Richard has insisted through the years that he did not know of either violation in victory lane, and he wondered how, even with an oversized engine, he had led just 23 of the 334 laps. His response at the time was, "If I have a big engine and the wrong tires, I'm going to finish second or third. That way, no one inspects my car."

"If I don't get the victory, who gets it?" he added. "How would anyone know for sure *that* car was legal?"

The gaffe, it should be noted, occurred at a time when many of the top teams were accused of cheating. Fingers had already been pointed at DiGard and Junior Johnson. Maurice Petty, who built the allegedly oversized engine, told reporters, in an indirect way, that he'd gotten tired of getting beat by the tricksters.

Regardless of the truth, the outcome at Charlotte damaged Richard's reputation, at least for a while, and opened a chasm between "The King" and Maurice. Pollard was discharged immediately afterward.

Then came the fatal blow—the 7-Eleven deal ended up including a requirement for the team switch to Ford cars. The team had a good inventory of Pontiacs from the previous year and seemed ready for the 1984 campaign. Suddenly, "we had to start all over," Kyle recalls.

After the 1984 season, Kyle "started over" again, leaving the Level Cross Shop to join up with the Wood Brothers team—the younger Wood brothers.

Glen Wood had founded a family dynasty equal to the Pettys' in the early 1950s; the Wood team, with David Pearson, had been the Pettys' fiercest rival through the 1970s because Leonard Wood was a natural genius with the Ford small block (introduced in 1974), making it work while the engines of others leaked and blew. Glen's sons, Eddie and Len, were contemporaries of Kyle; they'd grown up in racetrack infields—tossing footballs, horsing around, and talking racing. The 7-Eleven/Ford conundrum fell naturally into the Woods' hands, despite the apparent irony of Kyle's going to work for his father's oldest and greatest rivals.

"Eddie and I were straight-up from the very beginning," Kyle recalls. "I walked in the Wood Brothers' shop, and it was a mirror image of this shop in '84, '85. Everybody, their last name was Wood, or [they were] married to a Wood. I looked around and said, 'Eddie, here's the way it works: If you don't want me to drive, just tell me, because I know I'm the one who's going to be gone. You're not going to fire the crew chief; you're not going to fire the engine builder.' "

"My uncle ran this place for a year, with Dick Brooks and a couple of deals," Kyle adds. "Then my father ended up coming back in the next year or so.

"It was about eighteen months. We still built motors over here, still ran a few cars, ran six or seven races. But it was pretty much a ghost town compared to what it had been."

Racing is a tough business. In this 1979 photo, Richard greets Butch Lindley, NASCAR Late Model Sportsmen champ for the prior two seasons. A few years later, Butch was injured in an off-season race in Florida. After a five-year coma, he died in 1990. *Dick Conway*

Petty follows Cale Yarborough (11) and Dale Earnhardt (2) into Turn 1 at Martinsville in 1980. That year, Earnhardt won his first championship, with Petty sliding to fourth in the standings. Dale went on to win six more, equaling Petty's once-unapproachable record. *Dick Conway*

Team leader: Richard, unmistakable in his trademark hat, spends time with Kyle's youthful crew during preparations for the 1980 race at Charlotte. *Dick Conway*

During these years, "The King" raced in his standard blue car with red stripes while his son drove a red car with blue stripes. In an unusual pit road view from Richmond, the two Petty cars start the race nearly side by side. *Dick Conway*

Maurice Petty, with standard tools of the trade, works over an engine in the 1980s. *Dick Conway*

Crewman Wade Thornburg, with the Pettys almost from the start, helps push the car to the qualifying line. He was as much a rock in the Petty organization as Maurice and Dale Inman, and his death in 1985 was felt deeply throughout the organization. *Dick Conway*

Kyle looks over his No. 42 before the start of the Daytona 500 in 1981, at the start of his first full season in the majors. Engine trouble knocked him out of the race after 128 of the 200 laps. *Dick Conway*

Richard beats Kyle out of the pits during the 1981 Daytona 500. The boxy, pre-fastback cars almost resemble the design of NASCAR trucks, circa 2004.

Dick Conway

Richard won one last Daytona 500 in 1981 thanks to a gutsy call by Dale Inman. While other drivers pitted late in the race for gas and tires, Inman, timing the intervals to the second, went for a few seconds of fuel and Petty kept the lead, winning the race. *Dick Conway*

The crowd gathers quickly around Richard's winning car in victory lane at Daytona in 1981. The ceremonies during this era had an informal, respectful feeling to them. They were often happy and memorable moments, not time for a commercial break in the televised broadcast. *Dick Conway*

Richard consults with son Kyle in the pits at Richmond. *Dick Conway*

Opposite page: Amid the growing problems with fielding two teams, "The King" brought it home one more time at the Daytona 500, marking his 193rd career victory, at age 43. He also won that year at North Wilkesboro and Michigan. Few believed this Daytona 500 win, Petty's seventh, would be his last. *Dick Conway*

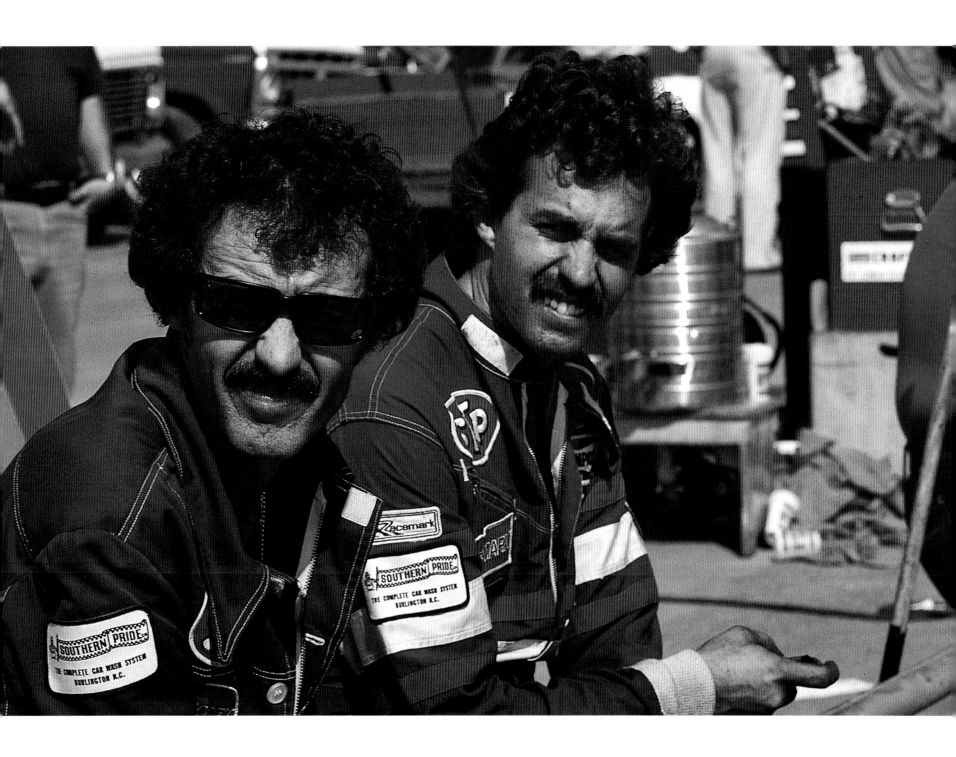

This picture almost begs you to look back at earlier shots of Richard and Lee, to see the flow of the generations. There are similarities between Richard and Kyle, and there are differences, much as there were in comparing Richard and his dad. *Dick Conway*

Opposite page: Even though Lee Petty was spending less and less time at the tracks in the early 1980s, he did make time to get a firsthand look at Kyle's progress. He didn't get that luxury with Adam, who made his first Cup start at Texas on April 2, 2000. Lee Petty, at the time lying in bed ill, died just three days later. *Bob Tronolone*

The lens enhances the view of the Petty cars garaged together at Daytona, with Richard, increasingly in the owner role, consulting with the crews. *Dick Conway*

Kyle and his wife, Pattie, at Bristol in 1981, a year after becoming parents. Their first child, Adam, was born on July 10, 1980. *Dick Conway*

Kyle and Richard in the pits at Richmond. Kyle, with one leg in the car, seems to be in a hurry to get on about his business. "The King," meanwhile, looks pretty businesslike with a shop rag in the right pocket.

Dick Conway

Kyle and Mike Beam look under the hood of the No. 42 car, while Richard waits to get back on the track during a practice. *Dick Conway*

The No. 42 and No. 43 cars side by side in the pits. *Dick Conway*

Incipient sponsorship from 7-Eleven helped ease the load on Petty Enterprises and STP in 1983. At the same time, it increased the urgency for Kyle to take off on his own. One omen was the arrival of Budweiser sponsorship, with Anheuser-Busch a major player in the growth of NASCAR's marketing strategy (behind Kyle, Terry Labonte is sporting Bud colors). *Dick Conway*

CHAPTER NINE

WINNING NO. 200 WITH THE GIPPER

———

"I guess if you would pick out
my twenty-fifth victory or thirtieth,
it wouldn't seem that important.
When I won my one hundredth race,
I don't think anyone made much noise about it."

Mike Curb found success early on in life. An independent record producer from California, he became a millionaire in his early 20s, starting his career writing advertising jingles for Honda motorcycles ("you meet the nicest people on a Honda" was one of his). His eye for talent led him to sign star acts like the Osmond brothers, Debby Boone, Shaun Cassidy, and Hank Williams Jr. before any one else did. He later branched into Christian music and established an office in Nashville, in part to establish independence from the Hollywood labels. He even found his way into politics, serving as California's lieutenant governor from 1978–1982.

Curb established his link with NASCAR after he realized the connection between racing fans and the type of music he produced. He wasn't content, though, to just make a few business connections in the sport. He became a car owner, one Richard Petty signed with for the launch of a new team in 1984.

In the winter of 1983-1984, Petty had talked with many owners about leaving Petty Enterprises. In fact, he almost signed with Rick Hendrick and the newly established Hendrick Motorsports—he came *that* close. He also talked with former car owner Butch Mock, who had a partnership with Bob Rahilly in the Rahmoc team.

"[Rahmoc] had good engines. They were dedicated and might need some guidance, but they were good guys. We went to Daytona and tested, getting ready for the season. That's how close it was; we made the commitment to them," Richard says. "I think Buddy [Parrott] was involved in it too. He was going to be the crew chief. We were going to take what we had and what they had and marriage it together. When we got down to the nitty-gritty between the lawyers and trying to work out the contract, it just fell through.

"Curb was involved in some way. I don't really remember how it all came together. The deal was, I took my race cars and my sponsor and went over there. We hired a bunch of new people because these [Petty] guys didn't want to go over there. . . . Buddy ran the operation; we got the shop together and the people together. We had a good crew, good people, good cars."

With his team in place, and with leased engines built by horsepower king Robert Yates at DiGard, Richard, 46, started to prepare for the 1984 season-opener at Daytona. His results during Speed Week were mixed. He had trouble in his qualifying heat and started 34th. He led 24 of the 200 laps, though, before he fell out with engine trouble just before the halfway mark.

He muddled through that spring, as he neither qualified nor finished particularly well. His cars were durable, yet Petty finished on the lead lap only once in the first 10 races. Richard's breakthrough came at Dover, where he led 129 of the 500 laps around the brutal mile oval and beat Tim Richmond by four seconds for victory number 199.

By this time, Richard was far and away ahead of anyone else in the number of wins column. His closest competition was his old rival David Pearson, who had 105 first-place finishes but was pretty much all-but retired from racing by then. Even the rest of the sporting world realized Petty's dominance. To baseball and football fans, he had the equivalent of 1,500 home runs or 100,000 rushing yards.

Now with an improbable 200th Petty win now just around the corner, the hype about his accomplishment was full blown—even though the stain of win number 198 the previous fall at Charlotte was still fresh. Everyone thought the big victory would come at the Memorial Day 600 at Charlotte, 80 miles from the Pettys' home lot. Vendors quickly worked up shirts and hats with the number 200 in various displays and did good business. Yet, the monumental moment would not come that day. All the anticipation came down in a crush when Petty had an engine blow after 216 laps.

True to a racer's mindset, Petty was much less preoccupied with the number than the public was. "I guess if you would pick out my twenty-fifth victory or thirtieth, it wouldn't

Petty admonishes a crewman before the start of a race at Charlotte; the transition was not without setbacks. *Dick Conway*

With Kyle driving the lone car at Petty Enterprises and "The King" out of the Level Cross shop, the entire hierarchy of motorsports had changed. Very suddenly, racing wasn't about the old guard anymore, and rising stars like Terry Labonte, who won the 1984 championship, were getting more attention. *Dick Conway*

seem that important," he explains. "When I won my one hundredth race, I don't think anyone made much noise about it. We just went on and won one hundred and one, and so on."

He told reporters at the time that the main significance of winning number 200 to him was "so you won't keep asking me about it and I can go on racing, and people will know I'm not going to retire when I get my two hundredth win in the books."

His performances at the following races at Riverside and Pocono were only fair, and at Michigan in June, he dropped out early with a broken fuel pump. Then, suddenly, all the stars in heaven aligned, one last time, for Richard Petty in July.

With 1984 being an election year, and NASCAR active in Republican politics, President Ronald Reagan had been invited to give the start command at the Firecracker/Pepsi 400 at Daytona on July 4, Independence Day, two days after Richard Petty's 47th birthday. Due to the president's schedule security and concerns, he had to arrive after the start of the race, so he gave the start command while flying in on Air Force One. After he actually was at the track, Reagan visited the broadcast booth and took a turn at the microphone with the Motor Racing Network (a half-century before, he briefly had been a radio sports announcer).

Then just when it couldn't get better, it did. Petty had led 50-some of the 157 laps, but he seemed to be a sitting duck, with Cale Yarborough and Harry Gant lined up behind for the traditional slingshot. But when Doug Heveron wrecked in the first turn on Lap 198, a caution was issued. Both Petty and Yarborough realized the race to the yellow was the race to the finish, and both attacked down the backstretch and into the final turn. Their cars sideswiped—Petty on the inside, Yarborough on the outside, and then they dragged to the finish line. Richard reached the flag by half a car.

That clinched it. In front of the president of the United States, and at NASCAR's number one racetrack, Richard Petty had won number 200. That seemed to complete a line that began with his father's legacy, his 1964 championship, his unmatched 1967 season, his 1976 battle with Pearson, his part in the 1979 television race at Daytona, and his seven championships—it all came together in one high-noon moment.

Then, almost as if destiny had concluded, the door shut. Engines broke at the next two stops, Nashville and Pocono. From Daytona to the end of the season, Richard did not lead a single lap, nor did he finish on the lead lap in any race. By the end of the year, he was 10th in points.

One thing that's never gotten much attention is how Richard's aptitude with cars contributed significantly to his success. Here he inspects under the front end of one of the Pontiacs. *Dick Conway*

As each race passed, it became more apparent that the Curb/Petty alliance wasn't working. Yet, Petty sweated out one more year with Curb. In 1985, he had 12 DNFs in 28 races, mostly due to mechanical failures, and led just 105 laps all year, the majority coming at Richmond in September, where he finished third, his best finish of the season. For most of the year, he had had no better than, maybe, a 10th-place car.

Kyle's was the only team in the Petty garage after his dad went to drive for Mike Curb. Here Kyle sits at a picnic table in the shop reading a racing paper as his car is prepped for an upcoming race. *Dick Conway*

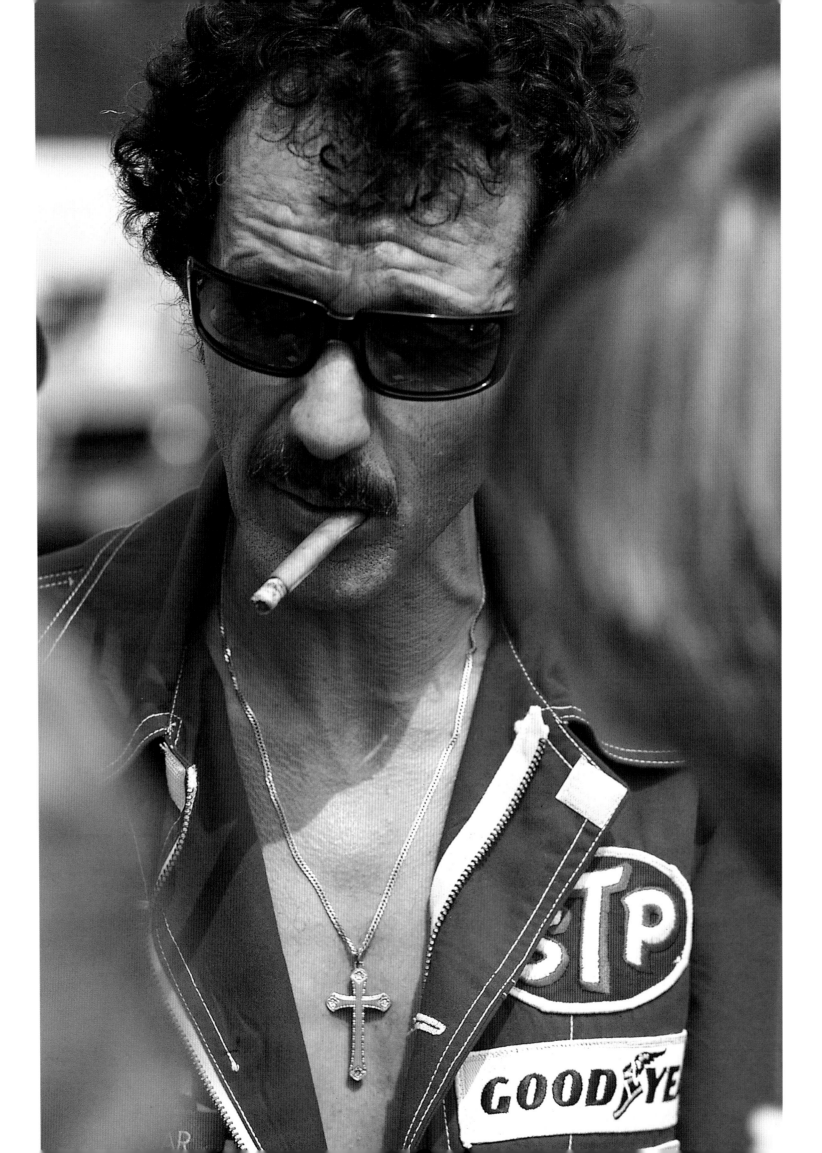

At far left, a hatless Petty chomps on a cigar while he chats with fans at Daytona. At right, he sports his more classic look while stroking his chin, one of his more well-known mannerisms. *Dick Conway*

Petty gets congratulatory kisses from the trophy queens after winning his 200th race, the Firecracker/Pepsi 400, at Daytona on July 4, Independence Day, in front of President Ronald Reagan. *The Daytona Beach News Journal*

A fan stands in awe just looking at the car of "The King." *Dick Conway*

The Petty pit crew works to cool down (with a garden hose, no less) the No. 43 car during one of the hottest Southern 500 races at Darlington on Labor Day. The year is 1983. *Dick Conway*

The 1980s cars were fascinating, as they show the evolution of NASCAR's stock cars into the spec cars of later decades. The change seemed to come suddenly, as spoilers sprouted and bumpers disappeared. This is Petty's car at Charlotte in 1984. *Dick Conway*

Opposite page: "The King" had plenty on his mind as the 1980s progressed. Kyle's career, the future of Petty Enterprises, his health, and his own driving plans all became pressing issues. *Dick Conway*

Dale Inman's tenure as crew chief for Terry Labonte produced a championship in 1984, confirming Inman's stature as a master of the game. *Dick Conway*

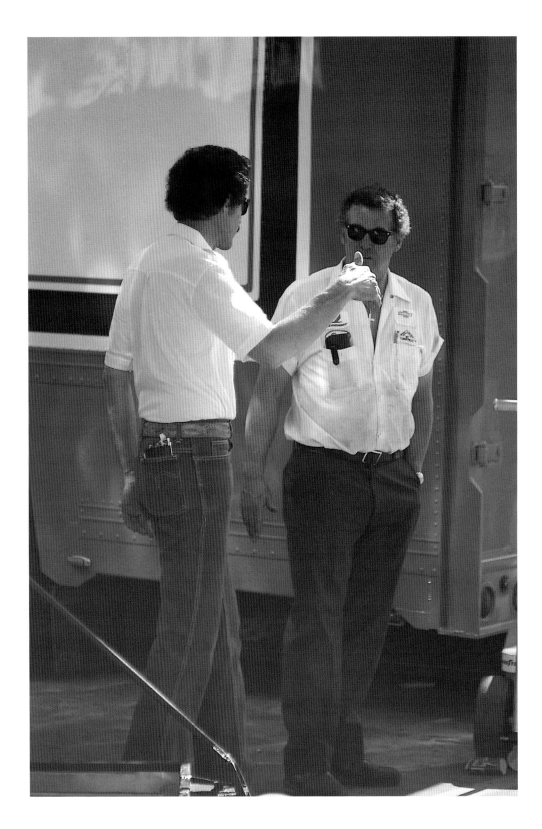

Despite the fact that Dale Inman left Petty Enterprises in early 1981, he and Richard remained close. Here, at Daytona in 1984, the cousins felt comfortable in consulting over a handling issue. *Dick Conway*

Inman, who had won four championships, coaches Labonte, then 27, in the garages at Daytona before the 1984 season, when Labonte won his first championship. The team was among only a number of competitors that hadn't significantly changed personell from the prior year. *Dick Conway*

Petty passes Dave Marcis at Richmond. Marcis, the ultimate independent, drove Butch Mock's No. 75 briefly in 1984. *Dick Conway*

After spending close to 25 years behind the wheel, Richard had seen the cockpit of the No. 43 go through many changes. *Dick Conway*

Richard with his daughter Lisa at Rockingham in 1984. By then, Lisa had become acquainted with Charlie Luck, a young engineer and aspiring racer. Lisa and Charlie later married, and Charlie became manager of the family's quarry business. Their first child, a son, was named after Richard. *Dick Conway*

Petty talks with a group of reporters at Charlotte in 1984. Note that everything from pens to typewriters—even a primitive computer—were being used as recording devices. *Dick Conway*

When Richard left to drive for Mike Curb in 1984, Buddy Parrott was hired as his crew chief. Both men were strong-willed and weren't familiar with the other's style. Nevertheless, Parrott guided Richard to his last two victories, including the epochal number 200 at Daytona in the summer. *Dick Conway*

Dave Marcis' wingtip shoes were perhaps the most-famous footware of the 1980s and 1990s. Most forget, though, that Petty always drove in his customary cowboy boots, shown here with heel shields attached and ready for action.

Racing and its competitors weren't the only aspects of NASCAR that had significantly changed by the mid-1980s. Tracks had started to become big-time commercial venues, with advertising signs replacing unadorned board fences. *Dick Conway*

Richard advises Charlie Luck, a racer in the Busch Series, who married Petty's daughter Lisa in the fall of 1987. *Dick Conway*

With "The King" gone, Maurice helped build engines for Kyle and kept his business running even after Kyle went to drive for the Woods. The door to his shop indicates you should stay out—unless you know you belong or have been invited. *Dick Conway*

A section of the parts stock at Petty Enterprises, with everything from rear-gear assemblies to spark plugs racked up in neat order.

CHAPTER TEN

WINNING WAYS COME TO AN END

—

"I wanted to get a good team together.
I knew one of these days
[that] I was going to have to step out of here,
and I wanted a good driver to carry on."

Mike Curb could give no firm assurances for success in 1986, so Richard, with his options dwindling, put the band back together at Level Cross. With Kyle safely established at the Wood Brothers, Petty reconciled with crew chief Dale Inman (who, incidentally, had won the championship with Terry Labonte in 1984) and brought STP back to home ground, in the classic red-and-blue No. 43 car.

Publicly, Richard was the same old Richard, bound and determined to win. "We know we're going to win races," "The King" said at the time. "We've done it before. A lot of them cats thinking they're going to win races have never done it." Yet in his own mind—*behind them sunglasses*—Richard knew he faced a long push up a long hill.

"We had to start a new engine program, start a new team," Richard says. "I was so busy concentrating on getting the business going that the driving stuff was sort of a sideline. I just sort of got in the car and drove and worried about the business, sort of like Kyle does now [with the twenty-first century Petty Enterprises]. I was too unfocused.

"Then they came with the new Pontiac in '87 with the crazy fastback deal [as opposed to the prior GM notchbacks] . . . which wasn't a whole lot better."

The result was a second nonwinning season in a row in 1986—the first time in Richard's career that he had failed to win in back-to-back years. His best finish in 1986 was second at Atlanta in the fall.

Certainly Richard believed that he *was* putting the band back together, and that the mediocre 1986 campaign was the first step in the revival of the one-time center of racing. Petty, however, is and was a realist. He saw the writing on the wall—or at least on the sides of the cars.

From the time of his injuries in 1961, Lee Petty was seen less and less at the racetrack, although he continued as owner of Petty Enterprises. He turned up here at Daytona in 1984 and consulted with Maurice in the garages. Maurice, at the time, was building engines for Kyle while Richard was driving for Mike Curb. *Dick Conway*

The sponsor dollars game had changed a lot since the days when the Pettys first brought the concept to the forefront of NASCAR in the early 1970s. Now instead of just STP, Purolator, Coke, and Pepsi, the sponsors of cars ranged from Coors and GM Goodrich to Folgers and Wrangler. These big corporations had come to see the emerging visibility of NASCAR racing and pitched a ton of money at those smart enough to catch it. Among those benefiting were men like Rick Hendrick, Harry Ranier, Richard Childress, and Jack

It's amazing how much drama NASCAR has built into things drivers and teams do routinely—getting gas, going to the tire shop. Here you can sense the urgency as the Petty team pushes the No. 43 car after a gas-and-go stop at Richmond in 1985. *Dick Conway*

Kyle, driving the Woods' No. 7, pushes Lennie Pond (49, driving for James Hylton) out of the way at Richmond in 1985. Pond, from Chester, Virginia, was one of those drivers who, if given the right breaks, could have been a contender. *Dick Conway*

Roush. Ford Motor Company also brought rejuvenated enthusiasm back to the racing scene by offering more support of its teams in 1984. Hence, GM had to ante up and get into the game too.

The Petty group, because of Richard's legendary loyalty to the brand and company, kept its sponsor deal with STP the same. But with all the other top-dollar sponsors out there, and their money buying more and more speed, the rest of the racing world sped past Petty Enterprises in a very short timespan. The same could be said of others among the sport's past legends—the Woods, Bud Moore—but the explosion hit the Petty team at a vulnerable time.

Kyle, Richard, and Lee spend some time in the old garages at Daytona in 1985. Note the careful markings on the sets of bias tires, which had to be measured and lined up with regard to stagger. *Dick Conway*

Kyle talks things over with Eddie Wood at Daytona. There was an easy coalition among the Petty and Wood teams, once fervent rivals. *Dick Conway*

Looking back, Kyle simply puts it this way: "You look at the Wood Brothers, you look at Childress, look at Petty Enterprises, Bud Moore. They were all major players in the sport, and they were at the top. What happened was not so much that these guys failed; it's that somebody came in and built on top of them.

"It's like Donald Trump building in New York. He bought the air space over top of us and built on top of us."

Still, Richard continued trying to do things the way he knew best.

"I was doing a lot of off-the-wall stuff with the car because I wanted to get a good team together," he says. "I knew one of these days [that] I was going to have to step out of here, and I wanted a good driver to carry on. So I was concentrating more on that than the driving deal.

Leonard Wood (left) and Eddie Wood look under the hood of the Woods' car at Daytona. Kyle, in the background, sits on his father's No. 43, talking to members of the STP crew. *Dick Conway*

"The financial deal was one problem. I tried to get that together, tried to get the car together. My big problem was that I just loved to drive a race car. I'd done it for thirty years. I loved to get in that car—nobody talking to you on the phone, the banker not wanting to be paid, somebody not complaining about something. You done your own thing, and it was hard to turn it loose because it was *me*."

The Petty team struggled through 1987, a carbon copy of 1986. Richard led something like 40 laps all season, with a best finish of second at Bristol in the spring. He was eighth in the points race, a little better than his 14th-place standing the previous year. But the dynasty had not even hit bottom yet. The worse was yet to come.

Petty qualified poorly for the 1988 Daytona 500, gridding 34th via the qualifying heats. He held his own midpack through the first half of the race, and then, with drastic suddenness,

Two legends: Petty runs side-by-side with A. J. Foyt at Daytona in 1986. Foyt, four-time Indy 500 winner and perhaps America's greatest racing star, ran regularly in the Daytona 500 from the 1960s to the 1990s, winning (with the Wood Brothers) in 1972. *Dick Conway*

Petty chases Dale Earnhardt through the east turn at Daytona in 1987. Earnhardt, at this point driving for Richard Childress, won his third championship that year and was on the way to equaling Richard's seven NASCAR titles. *Dick Conway*

Petty, with barely time to slip out of his gear, speaks with Motor Racing Network reporter Jerry Punch after falling out of another race. Punch later migrated from radio to TV and was one of the dependable broadcast reporters during NASCAR's pre-network age. *Dick Conway*

his blue-and-red Pontiac flipped wildly into the air and tumbled over and over—five, six, seven, who knows how many flips—before coming to rest on its feet. The final blow came in the form of a broadside hit from Brett Bodine, who had nowhere to go.

It was the worst crash that many fans and members of the media had ever seen. Motorsports writers sat stunned in the press room for moments before they headed en masse to the infield hospital. Amazingly, Petty was not badly hurt. "I closed my eyes, held my breath, and then everything went black," Petty recalls. He came out of it with only a badly bruised foot.

"Everything I've got is still working," Richard says, half-amazed now that he's pushing 70. "I don't hurt. I guess it's a lot of good genes and a lot of good luck . . . . I've been more than fortunate. I had the cancer [prostate], and they cut that out and throwed it away. I got like seven doctors, and they check everything from your toenails to your hair—a specialist for everything. I went up there, I'm sixty-six years old, and they tell me I'm in good shape for a fifty-four-year-old man.

"So I come back and tell them girls in there [the Petty offices] I'm fifty-four years old."

Yet Petty's legendary good health and good nature couldn't protect him from the worst blow of all, in 1989, when his legendary record of running 513 races in a row—which has now been surpassed by Terry Labonte and Ricky Rudd—came to an end at Richmond that winter. There he failed to make speed in the first round of qualifying, which set the top 20 (NASCAR at the time allowed for two rounds of time trials). In the second round, Petty hit the wall. At the time, 36 cars started at Richmond, with two provisional spots based on points. Those two provisional openings went to Davey Allison and Dave Marcis.

So as the sun set over the old half-mile, a somber feeling settled in among the crowd as Petty, in his characteristic cowboy hat and sunglasses—a reflection of lovely days in victory lanes—went to the NASCAR office to consult with series directors Les Richter and Dick Beaty. It didn't look good.

Finally, Richard came out, looked around the crowd of reporters waiting, and said, "I'm going home, guys." He walked to his hauler and ordered his men to load it up.

Back in the old days of show-up money and promoter deals, NASCAR had always found ways to include its biggest stars in the show, but now it seemed to have come to a point where Richard Petty didn't matter any more. Procedures were procedures; no exceptions allowed.

"That was as down as I ever felt, aside from losing a couple of people," Richard says somberly. "We didn't run fast enough the first day, and the second day was slower and we didn't make the race. The cut-off was 36 cars, and I think we were 37th, and at that time there was nothing in the rulebook, nothing they could come up with, to extend the deal."

Other drivers, notably Rodney Combs, who qualified 21st on speed in the second round, offered Richard their qualified cars, so as to keep the streak alive, to keep the legend in the show, but Richard refused.

In 1987, NASCAR allowed teams to use fastback GM cars in an attempt to allow aerodynamic equality with the low, slick Fords. The so-called notchbacks were given a sweep of rear glass from the back of the roof to the spoiler. A few were made for the street, but this was the beginning of the end for stock requirements. *Dick Conway*

"He said, 'Just take my car, keep the record.' " Petty remembers. "I said no. If I can't run my crap, I ain't running it. That's how hard-headed I was. It was principles. . . . We came, we did the best we could, and we didn't make it. You got to have a stopping point somewhere."

Missing at Richmond brought doom in the points, which determined the optional provisionals at the end of the field. Although the main problem was that the Petty cars simply were not fast enough on pole day, the points situation also left him with no recourse when the back-mark spots were filled. Petty missed three more races on the same grounds through the rest of 1989, making just 25 of the 29 scheduled events.

NASCAR eventually rectified the situation, instituting the "champion's provisional"—a spot reserved for any active former champion. On that April day at Richmond, and for the rest of the 1989 season, it was too little, too late.

The "Petty provisional" is now a weird footnote in NASCAR history. It prolonged the career of Darrell Waltrip, who used dozens of champ spots as he faded in the late 1990s. As NASCAR has grown and as the old champs retire, it's become moot, but it's still in the rulebook. That maybe is a small measure of what Richard Petty has meant to the game, in the end.

Petty buzzes by newcomer Ernie Irvan at Daytona in 1988. Ernie, driving this year for D. K. Ulrich, grew to be one of NASCAR's most exciting and talented stars in the 1990s, before serious injuries cut his career short. *Dick Conway*

General Motors introduced its new line in 1988, with Pontiac leading with its Grand Prix. The Grand Prix earned great prestige with Rusty Wallace and Penske in 1993 and 1994. *Dick Conway*

The Petty personality never changed, through triumph, failure, and tragedy. "The King" remained, and remains, a steadfast rock to his fans, even as the graph of success rose and fell around him. *Dick Conway*

End of the line? Petty contemplates his failure to qualify at Richmond in February 1988, ending a then-record streak of 513 consecutive races. NASCAR, under its criteria, could find no way for Petty to make the grid, and Richard, for the first time in his career, loaded up and went home. *Dick Conway*

CHAPTER ELEVEN

FINAL TOUR
FOR THE FANS

—

"I'd seen too many people drive a race car,
get out of a race car,
then try to get back in.
So I said,
'There ain't no second chance at this thing.'"

When talking about a great sports hero, no one likes to spend too much time talking about his eventual decline and fall, even in the case of a legend who hung on far past what his reputation could sustain. Richard Petty doesn't deny that he kept racing longer than he needed to, but says he did hang it up on better terms than others did. "[Darrell Waltrip] went a lot further down than I did," Petty notes, referring to Waltrip's long-awaited retirement tour in 2000.

Speculation about Petty's retirement started about 10 years before he ended his racing career in 1992. The problem for Richard was that he couldn't figure a decent way out. For a while, sure, he believed he could rejuvenate Petty Enterprises. But by 1990, he knew that his 53-year-old body was beat up too badly to rebound, and his business responsibilities far outweighed what he could do in a car.

It was a hard decision to face, though. No competitor likes to look in the mirror and say he isn't what he used to be. It's a much longer fall for the superheroes. A decade later, superstars such as Bill Elliott, Ricky Rudd, Terry Labonte, Rusty Wallace, and Mark Martin would all face the same question Petty did in the early 1990s: When do you know it's time?

Petty, always willing to give a tip to anyone who asked, counsels an unidentified driver through the window. *Dick Conway*

"That's a hard one to answer," said Rudd, ultimate successor to Petty as NASCAR's all-time "Iron Man," with a streak of consecutive races well past 800. "In 2002 [with Robert Yates], we were like sixth in points and had won a couple races. In 2003 [with the Wood Brothers], we were twenty-something in points and hadn't really come close.

"You start to wonder, 'Is it me? Is it the team? Is it a combination?' I can't believe I went from being able to drive a race car one year and not being able to the next. But you start to wonder about everything."

"Don't get me wrong, I still enjoy driving race cars, and I think I'm a better driver than I was ten years ago," Elliott said shortly before announcing his "retirement" at the end of 2003. "But you get to a point where all the things that go with it start to wear you down."

Primary among such things for Richard was the fact that he was responsible, even in the decade as his career declined, for a good-sized company, where dozens of people worked and depended upon the success of that company for their livelihoods.

"I had to keep the company going, to keep *me* going, to keep all the people working for us going, keep the sponsors going," he says. "Most drivers aren't that way. They're just part of a team. I *was* the team. So if I left, there would have been nothing here. There were a lot of people, but who would run it? I was the glue. When the glue leaves, the pieces fall apart.

"Yet, eventually, I said, 'Hey, one of these days STP is going to say time-out guys, you ain't getting the job done.' So I said I'd better get out before it's too late.

"I'd seen too many people drive a race car, get out of a race car, then try to get back in. So I said, 'There ain't no second chance at this thing,' know what I mean? So OK, in doing that I [decided that] I'd rather overstay my welcome . . . get as many years as I could before

By the early 1980s, when this portrait was taken, Richard's best years were behind him. There was still something of a gunslinger in him, though. *Dick Conway*

I made the announcement," he adds. "I knew in my mind what I was going to do—wind myself down, try to get in the deal where, hey, I'm coming down off the mountain, fellows."

Finally, on October 1, 1991, with five decades of racing in his pocket, and with a lifetime devoted to the sport, Richard Petty made his momentous and gut-wrenching announcement: the 1992 season, dubbed "The Fan Appreciation Tour," would be his last.

That was a typical Petty touch. He could have called it "Richard's Last Ride," or "Farewell to The King," but he didn't. From the time he began racing as a gawky teenager to his rank as senior statesman, Richard Petty always had a keen appreciation of the people who have made him go from Richard Petty to *Richard Petty, "The King."*

That day probably was more emotional for the rest of the Petty family than it was for Richard, who seldom shows his internal emotions. Wife Lynda had been quietly urging Richard to step aside for years, especially after the terrifying crash at Daytona in 1988, but

even she felt conflicted about the reality of his days as a driver coming to an end. You see, racing wasn't just Richard's life—it was Lynda's too, as well as his family's.

"I probably have encouraged him [to quit] every week," Lynda said at the time. "But all of the sudden, after next year [1992], I wonder what we're going to do, if we can sit there and watch without the forty-three out there.

"I probably feel like I sacrificed a lot," she continued. "I think he was around for one child's birth; the rest of the time he was racing. He missed most all of the graduations, the banquets, the recitals, and all. He missed it all. . . . But my philosophy is that I'm just thankful I've been a part of Richard Petty's life, and no matter what happens from this day forth, I can look back without any regrets."

To critics, Petty's final tour seemed silly and contrived.

"Here's where people who try to analyze the last few years of his career miss the picture," son Kyle says. "The first twenty or thirty years of his career, that was for *you*. The last four or five years, that was for *him*. He enjoyed driving a race car. He enjoyed going to the

Petty had visibly begun to fade by 1990. Although he made all the races that year, thanks to the so-called "Petty provisional" instituted after his DNQ at Richmond, he failed to finish 12 of the 29 events. Here, he trails Morgan Shepherd (15) and Dave Marcis (71) on the inside at Charlotte. Ricky Rudd (5) and Davey Allison (28) are on the outside. *Dick Conway*

Richard lines up at Daytona in 1992 behind Phil Parsons (9) and ahead of Terry Labonte (94) and Ernie Irvan (4). *Dick Conway*

racetrack. He enjoyed seeing Steve Hmiel and guys who had worked here go on and work on other teams and be successful. He enjoyed being around Dale Earnhardt and Bill Elliott, seeing those guys come along at twenty-eight or twenty-nine and kick butt like he had done.

"He never crawled out of that car, even if he finished thirty-fifth, and said, 'I don't like doing this; I had a bad day.' "

In the end, The Fan Appreciation Tour proved to be a brilliant marketing concept—one in which the Petty team planned special appearances, events, and displays on the STP cars at each track, at each race to commemorate the career of "The King." The team also had small-scale toy cars minted to represent each event. (This was the beginning of the so-called "die-cast" boom, which grew into a highly profitable industry in the late 1990s and beyond.)

Petty made a lot of money from these promotions—another point that had the critics howling—but he deserved it. It took Richard Petty 13 years to make a million dollars in racing, while Jeff Gordon netted $70 million in winnings and untold millions in promotional deals in 10 years on the track. And if you look at the all-time money list, Petty isn't even close, with something like $7.75 million, 46th on the list. The racers ahead of him include Kenny Wallace, Mike Skinner, Joe Nemechek, John Andretti, Jeremy Mayfield, and Michael Waltrip. Yes, times did change from when NASCAR was a fledgling sport to when some of these racers hit the track and a lot more money was around. But then it seems almost heathen to begrudge Petty a dime.

Richard has no regrets about any of his earnings. "We ran Atlanta or something in the spring [of 1971], and I finally went over a million dollars for my whole life, and this was winning two or three championships and over one hundred races, OK? That's how much it paid at that particular time. Now they run one race and pay a million dollars. When we look at racing, we look at money and the whole deal, and we see how much that's escalated. . . . Baseball, football—[all sports] have all escalated. They was ahead of us, and they're still ahead of us. They went up ten percent, and we went up ten percent, but we're still fifty percent behind."

Yet Richard laughs about it all—without bitterness—having made his point.

Money matters aside, only one race was really memorable from The Fan Appreciation Tour: the Pepsi 400 at Daytona, where once again a president (this time George Bush) was there to see history unfold. Daytona always held some kind of magic for Petty—who had won seven Daytona 500s and five other races there—and it sparked again when he set a top time in the qualifying run. Much to the roaring crowd's displeasure, though, Sterling Marlin, driving for Junior Johnson, later beat Petty for the pole. Many groaned

that Sterling hadn't gotten the message: "The King" was *supposed* to win the pole in his last Daytona start. Poor Sterling, a Tennessee country boy, said he never believed he'd be so badly booed for doing what he ought to do.

Saturday's main event fell apart for Petty, who started second and led the first few laps. He quickly fell back in the pack after that, and after 84 laps, he had to quit—the official cause being "driver fatigue."

"They had me up at about eight o'clock [not good for a notoriously late-riser], doing all these autographs, doing all the interviews, doing all the crap," Richard says. "I qualified second, but anyhow, we started and I led the first four or five laps. Then they got by me and got going. I ran fifteen or twenty laps and my tongue was hanging out. I was just totally exhausted. We just stopped. I was physically, mentally, just used up."

The end, of the season and Petty's career, finally came at Atlanta, then a 1.5-mile true oval where "The King" had won six times. True to Petty form, the Atlanta event held a lot of significance—but not only because it was the last race for a top racing legend. It also resolved one of the closest points races in NASCAR history (with long-shot Alan Kulwicki prevailing for the championship), and it was the first race for Indiana newcomer Jeff Gordon, who would take the baton and carry it far into the future.

Petty was never a contender in his finale. He had to take a provisional to start, and he was a lap or two behind when his race ended. On the 96th lap (of 328), Ken Schrader and Dick Trickle bumped and wrecked, gathering up Darrell Waltrip, Wally Dallenbach, and "The King" in the melee. Petty's car caught fire (you can see it, as it is and was, at the Petty Museum in Randleman), yet Petty, spitting smoke, drove it to the pits.

"The King" remained the center of attention for the press, on good days and bad, and he always obliged. Here Winston Kelley (at Petty's right) has the Motor Racing Network mike in the garage. *Dick Conway*

The Petty crew counts down a pit stop during the fall race at Charlotte in 1991. This turned out to be one of Richard's better days that season—he finished 12th. He finished even stronger at Richmond (11th) and at Watkins Glen (9th) that year. *Nigel Kinrade*

Dale Inman and crew worked the car for over an hour, all realizing the importance of a last lap. Finally, with a few to go, Richard came out of the pits in his scorched No. 43 and made the final couple of laps. He finished his final race, 232 laps behind, but he *finished*.

"I went out in a blaze," Richard says, chuckling, in a characteristic comment. "You'd like to go out in a blaze of glory, but I just went out in a blaze.

"I said [to the team], 'Guys, that's it.' They said, 'No, we're going to make you run that last lap.' So they went back and rebuilt the car, knocked the coolers off it, the fenders, the radiator.

"I went up in the truck, and here comes my daughters, my wife. They cried for fifteen minutes. They was happy it was over with, but they was sad because it was over with—a bunch of mixed emotions.

"I was glad that year was over with. If you'd been writing a script, you'd go out winning the race. We *knew* better. That just brought it all back down—this is real life. I did a final lap, a victory lap, waved at all the fans, and then it was over. Where are we going now? You ain't going back. That's it."

The simultaneous celebrations, Kulwicki as champion and Petty as "The King," seemed to coincide appropriately. No one had expected Kulwicki—long-shot independent from Wisconsin—to win the championship. And no one ever had expected there to be NASCAR without Richard Petty.

Richard was "supposed" to win the pole for his last start at Daytona, the 1992 Pepsi/Firecracker. However, Sterling Marlin (22) beat him by a fraction and started No. 1. Petty led the first lap, then fell back quickly and parked, exhausted, after 84 laps. *Nigel Kinrade*

When Richard Petty began his driving career in the sport of stock car racing, most of the tracks were only small, flat dirt ovals carved out of the countryside. When he ended his career, after seven Cup championships and 200 wins, NASCAR had large, high-banked tracks that would swell with spectator counts larger than most cities. These tracks, including Lowe's Motor Speedway, also are surrounded by corporate suites and commercial developments, including high-rise condominums. *Dick Conway*

Petty and Mark Martin try to hold the low line at well-aged Rockingham, where Martin scored his first Cup win in 1989. Petty had helped to open the track in 1965. In his last tour in 1992, he finished 16th and 25th in the two events there. *Nigel Kinrade*

Richard coasts alone to the No. 43 pit
marker in front of a huge crowd at
Daytona, ready, finally, to step out of the car.
Dick Conway

CHAPTER TWELVE

MOVING ON

—

"I've been doing this so long
it's hard not to go to the races.
I don't do nothing, but I'm there."

Previous Page: Coach's view: Petty, now managing from the dugout, keeps in touch via headset with driver Bobby Hamilton in 1995. Hamilton gave the Petty team a brief surge of enthusiasm with wins at Phoenix (1996) and Rockingham (1997). *Nigel Kinrade*

The man had come down from the mountain, but he really wasn't sure what to do next. He wasn't the first retired racing great to feel at a loss, though. Mario Andretti and Johnny Rutherford had faced the same dilemma; two years later, in 1994, the eternally restless A. J. Foyt would be in the same spot. But unlike Foyt, his contemporary, Richard kept his emotions and sentiments hidden under his big, plumed cowboy hat, even though most observers could tell he had a tough time adjusting to living on the ground.

"I couldn't just walk away from it," Petty admits. "I had to sort of work my way through it, trying to work my way out of this deal. I've been doing this so long it's hard not to go to the races. I don't do nothing, but I'm there."

Petty hence retreated to the role he'd taken when his father was hurt in 1961, as owner and leader of Petty Enterprises, but he had a huge hole in his heart. Kyle, his son and closest companion, wasn't working in the Level Cross shop.

"When he retired from driving a race car . . . part of him died; he's not one hundred percent the same guy he was," Kyle says now, years after he rejoined the Petty Enterprises fold. "There was a part of him he had to take and lock in a box and say, 'That's not who I am anymore. I'm not a race car driver. I'm a *retired* race car driver.' "

Yet Petty did keep busy, profiting from several sideline businesses—some of which were offshoots of The Fan Appreciation Tour. The most notable was the Richard Petty Driving Experience, a program that conducts driving schools at several tracks, giving racing hopefuls

Even in silhouette, there's no question of identity here. *Nigel Kinrade*

Richard and Kyle talk in the garages at Daytona in 1993, Richard's first post-retirement visit to the 500-mile race. Kyle was driving for Felix Sabates at the time and was on the way to one of his better seasons, finishing fifth in points. His best years on the track, 1989–1996, came during his stint with Sabates. *Nigel Kinrade*

a chance (for a couple thousand dollars) to try their hands at the wheel of Cup-type cars, with instructors along for the ride.

Still, getting the Petty Enterprise team back on the road to success was his main objective. In a surprise choice, he turned over the seat of the No. 43 car in 1993 to journeyman Rick Wilson, a husky kid from Florida who so far had had a nondescript career with several teams. Wilson finished a disappointing 28th in the points that year and did not return for the next season.

Many followers of racing certainly expected more, but from a realist's view, Petty Enterprises and its cars were not very good at the time of Richard's retirement. Petty wasn't going to get, say, Ricky Rudd or Terry Labonte or Jeff Gordon. In addition to the scarcity

Dale Earnhardt succeeded Richard Petty as NASCAR's top champion. Here the two men mix opinions at the 1994 closing race at Atlanta, where Earnhardt clinched his seventh Winston trophy. *Nigel Kinrade*

of talent, NASCAR had begun to attract a surplus of powerful new owners—Roger Penske, Jack Roush, Felix Sabates, Rick Hendrick, and Joe Gibbs. All brought new business approaches and factory partnerships to the game, and the Petty team more and more appeared shabby and dilapidated in its 1970s clothing.

A major issue impeding Petty Enterprises' success was money. Richard had a reputation for being tight with the dollars. It was a business model he had adhered to since his youth and it had worked for 30 years.

"This place has always had a knock—that we didn't spend money in the right place, that we didn't spend money on salaries, didn't do this, and didn't do that," Kyle says, face-front. "Part of the criticism is true, and I'll take part of that criticism. From standing

Bobby Hamilton (left) poses with "The King" after Hamilton's win at Rockingham in 1997. *Nigel Kinrade*

Darrell Waltrip, visibly older than at the time of his youthful battles with "The King," compares spark plugs with Petty at Dover in 1995. Waltrip had spun off his own team from the Rick Hendrick organization in 1989. His retirement tour came in 2000, eight years after Petty's. *Nigel Kinrade*

on the outside, being in Felix Sabates' operation, seeing what he was spending, where he was spending money and we were spending money, I'll take a little bit of that."

Of course, Petty Enterprises wasn't the only member of the old guard struggling in the rapidly changing NASCAR market. The Woods had fallen long and hard from their dominance in the 1960s and 1970s. Even Junior Johnson, who for years more or less brokered important transactions in NASCAR (including the Winston sponsorship in 1971), eventually took the back door out, selling the remains of his operation to Brett Bodine in 1994.

"The model just changed, and we didn't change with the model," Kyle says. "So when I came back to Petty Enterprises, we all had a lot of in-depth good-time discussions, heated discussions, about where I thought we should go and where he thought it should go. When the model changes and you don't change, then you're instantly behind. All you do from that point on is fall further behind. Once you're put in that position, you not only have to catch up, [but] you have to catch up and get ahead again."

Catching up was an agonizing process—one that took more than a decade. Driver Wally Dallenbach became part of Petty Enterprises in 1994, saw the shambles, and split with the group midyear. John Andretti took over for the rest of the season.

Tennessee veteran Bobby Hamilton brought stability to the organization in 1995, and he stuck it out for three years. He also gave Petty Enterprises its first victory since 1984 with a gutsy win at Phoenix in the fall of 1996. Hamilton also won two poles that year, at Michigan (June) and at Martinsville (September). The next year, 1997, rugged Hamilton won at Rockingham in the fall, with poles at Pocono and Phoenix. After the season, he

left to join Larry McClure. It was a pretty good run, and both driver and team had reason to be proud of it.

Also, in 1997, the dynasty began taking turns toward home. Kyle set up his pe2 subsidiary in Concord, North Carolina, 80 miles from Level Cross leaving his place as a driver for colorful billionaire Felix Sabates. The old connection with Mattel had turned fruitful, with Kyle receiving backing from the company's Hot Wheels brand. And while both Pettys more or less denied any connection between the two companies, most observers had some idea what was going on—and what was going to happen eventually.

The key to Kyle's homecoming was the fourth-generation Petty driver—his son Adam, then just 16. He had begun racing karts and was headed toward competing in the American Speed Association (ASA), the Midwestern short-track series that also begat the likes of Rusty Wallace, Mark Martin, Alan Kulwicki, and others. Meanwhile, his natural ability and spirit were starting to emerge and the racing world couldn't help but notice.

"What made me leave Felix was all about Adam and all about my family," Kyle explains. "I said, 'OK, I've got two sons. If they want to drive, it's not going to happen for them at Sabates'.

Kyle, having left Felix Sabates, had set up his own team for 1997—part of his long journey back to Petty Enterprises. Kyle's pe2 team eventually meshed back into the family business in 1999. Here Kyle solicits advice from "The King" at the 1997 Daytona opener. *Nigel Kinrade*

Richard, physically relaxed as always, tunes his eyes and mind on timing the cars on the track at Talladega in 1999. The back of the director's chair shows a promo for the Pettys' driving school. *Nigel Kinrade*

The newest Petty, and the future of the family company, 18-year-old Adam grew up at the tracks. Here he talks with his legendary grandpa at Talladega in 1998. Adam had shown some ability in short-track races at this time, and the family was preparing him for a shot at the top. *Nigel Kinrade*

Again, the torch is passed from one Petty to the next. After Lee brought Richard along, Richard made way for Kyle to make his racing debut. Here Kyle is doing the same for Adam at Daytona in 1999. *Nigel Kinrade*

He doesn't have time to step back and bring somebody along. So I left Felix and started my own deal, pe2.

"It was two separate entities, but through '97 and into '98, it just started getting closer and closer, so it was a natural thing to say, 'Let's go back, put the two Cup cars here, and Adam's thing we'll call pe2.' So Adam's program always was pe2."

By now Petty Enterprises, with Hamilton, had begun to show signs of life, and with Adam on the horizon, there was hope for a fresh start and a new approach. Adam moved up to the second-line Busch Series in 1998 with tentative (later full-speed) sponsorship from Sprint, one of a wave of new, high-tech companies that had recently brought sponsor dollars to the sport. Adam progressed to full-time driving in 1999, with major plans looming for 2000. The results weren't particularly impressive, but time would tell the tale. This was the future.

With the Pettys, family and business have never been separated—one always has been part of the other. Best-selling author Jerry Bledsoe recalls a time in the late 1970s, maybe early 1980s (around the time when Adam was born), when he observed the Petty clan loading up the van for a Sunday morning trip to the races at Martinsville. Among those along for the ride were Richard, Lynda, Martha Jane Bonkemeyer, daughter Sharon, and the babies in their safety seats. Richard drove an hour to the track and once he arrived, he headed off to the garage area to work. His family joined with the other racing broods out there, gathering in Martinsville's homey infield for what amounted to a glorified Sunday picnic.

That's how Adam spent many Sundays in his childhood, with other youngsters such as Jon Wood (Eddie Wood's son), Justin Labonte (Terry's boy), Brian Vickers, and the rest of the lads. He'd watch as Kelley Earnhardt (Dale's daughter) tossed a football with his brother Austin while cars noisily circled the 500 laps.

Adam eventually became a skinny 19-year-old, more the pattern of his grandfather, with the characteristic Petty grin and people-loving demeanor. By 2000, he was running the Busch Series full time and gaining on it. With Sprint sponsorship, he made his first Cup start at Texas in April 2000. He qualified the car, starting 33rd, but his engine gave out after 215 laps, leaving him 40th in his first and only Cup start.

A month later came the stunning news: Adam Petty was dead. He was killed, apparently instantly, in a crash during practice for the Busch race at New Hampshire Speedway on May 12, 2000. For weeks afterward, time stopped.

"It just stopped our world for a while," Richard says. "Then you've got to start over with a clean sheet of paper and just work your way from there."

The blow fell hardest, of course, on Kyle, who said he considered Adam not only his son but his best friend.

Kyle took off the next race at Charlotte. At Dover the following week, he and wife Pattie stood up to the microphones to tell the world of their grief.

"The accident happened on a Friday, and [daughter] Montgomery Lee and I were in London," Kyle said, his voice breaking occasionally. "I spent so much time with Adam at

Adam got a taste of victory lane when he was about six months old; his grandfather hoisted him above his head after winning the 1981 Daytona 500. *Dick Conway*

the racetrack [that] I felt like I needed to spend more time with Montgomery Lee and Austin, so I'd gone to London.

"Mike Helton [NASCAR president] called [with the news]. I couldn't tell Montgomery Lee when we were in England. I had to keep it from her for about 24 hours, until we got back. From that day on, we've lived in our own little world.

"It's been incredibly hard for Pattie and me to go back to Adam's race shop. You'll never know how hard it was to walk through those doors and see those cars sitting there with his name on it . . . his uniforms and stuff like that."

"This is what we always have done as a family," he added. "My father did it, my grandfather did it. I've done it, Adam did it. It's what we do. . . . Just because something goes bad or something goes wrong, you don't quit, you keep plugging along at it."

Probably the greatest result from that never-quit attitude has been the establishment of Kyle's Victory Junction Gang Camp, a hospice for children with severe illnesses and incurable diseases. It was something Adam wanted, and in the long run, the camp may be the most benevolent and lasting result of the Pettys' six decades in racing. It is based on other camps that Adam had visited in Florida and Connecticut. He had discussed plans for a similar effort, with the family setting aside acreage on the Petty property at Level Cross to be used, eventually, for the purpose.

Adam's death made the project come true. Kyle and Pattie redoubled efforts to get the job up and running, and via Kyle's annual cross-country motorcycle fund-raiser and other donations, the camp had $15 million in donations by the time it opened in the spring of 2004. It has full medical facilities, a lake, and a specially designed swimming pool, as well as facilities for horseback riding, arts and crafts, amateur plays, even a race shop, called Adam's Race Shop, where youngsters can get the feel of tools, machinery, and computers used on Cup cars.

"We saw it as a way for us to use it as part of a healing process and to find peace with Adam's accident," Kyle says. "These kids have hemophilia, sickle-cell, HIV, cancer, asthma, arthritis. Most of the kids are known at school as 'the sick kid.' Here, they can feel like they belong, for a change."

But getting back to racing has been tougher. The future of Petty Enterprises was resting on Adam and rebuilding that future has continued to elude this family with racing in its blood. Petty Enterprises has only scored three victories since Richard's team wins in 1983. Yet, "The King" remains hopeful, convinced that 2004 was a turning year for the team.

"It's definitely improved since last year," he said in May 2004 to the Associated Press. "Some of our finishes might not have been any better than last year, but the cars are definitely making the fields a little bit better, running a little bit better as the race goes on."

"The combination is just not going to come together all at one time. You just keep plugging away."

"[The team] is not down on each other or worrying about whatever's going on," he added. "They all want to be winners. Hopefully, one of these days we can make them all winners."

Adam Petty, ready for business, at Darlington in March 1999. His results from that first season were only fair, but he did show an aptitude toward running well at a number of tracks, including placing sixth at Daytona, a season-best fourth at Fontana, and fifth at Nazareth. *Nigel Kinrade*

Opposite Page: Adam helps the crew push his car toward the starting line at Bristol in April 1999. This was Adam's first full season, and he made his season-best start at this race after qualifying third. *Nigel Kinrade*

The Pettys' grand plan on display at Charlotte: Veteran Jimmy Hensley drove the truck, John Andretti had just won at Martinsville in the No. 43 car, Kyle raced the No. 44 Hot Wheels car, and the No. 45 was being ramped up for Adam. *Nigel Kinrade*

There's no mistaking the look. Adam's eyes were more his grandfather's than his father's, but his grin was a family trait. *Nigel Kinrade*

Trying to carry on after Adam's death was very difficult for everyone at Petty Enterprises. Both Richard and Kyle were experiencing immense personal grief, as well as concern over the future of the team. *Nigel Kinrade*

Opposite page: The face of "The King," weathered from each hard-earned victory—all 200. *Nigel Kinrade*

Kyle took the No. 45 car in honor of Adam, and he secured sponsorship from Georgia-Pacific in 2003. The Pettys also held open a door for former CART racer Christian Fittipaldi, who ran 16 races for the group in 2002 and 2003. That gave the Pettys connections to the Woods, the Andrettis, and the Fittipaldis. *Nigel Kinrade*

Think back to the look of Lee Petty's Plymouth coupe in 1950, then fast forward to 2004—where Kyle has enough gear and equipment behind the wheel to manage a space launch. *Nigel Kinrade*

REFLECTING ON HIS LEGACY

——

"I'm not special or nothing.
I was the guy who got lucky enough
to do what I got to do."

Petty's characteristic look has had several transitions, including the jaunty glasses and cheroot of the early and mid-1970s. *Dick Conway*

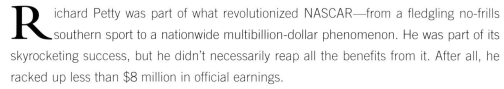

ichard Petty was part of what revolutionized NASCAR—from a fledgling no-frills southern sport to a nationwide multibillion-dollar phenomenon. He was part of its skyrocketing success, but he didn't necessarily reap all the benefits from it. After all, he racked up less than $8 million in official earnings.

When he reflects back, he doesn't regret his role, though—or the pressure that came with it. "I came in exactly at the right time for Richard Petty, for his circumstances, and for NASCAR racing. It fit in perfectly with the life, the society I was throwed into," he says. "I was just lucky. I was born in the right place at the right time with the right people and under the right circumstances. It wasn't a charmed life, but it was what I was trying to accomplish."

To Richard, his life came out the way God and nature intended. He looks back at his 35 years in a lethal business, one which took the lives of many of his contemporaries, friends, and family—Fireball Roberts, Joe Weatherly, Tiny Lund, Neil Bonnett, Randy Owens, Dale Earnhardt, and in the end, Adam Petty—and considers himself fortunate.

"It's the most unhealthy thing you can do," he says of racing. "I had a couple broke necks, two or three broke shoulders, broke fingers, broke the feet—you name it, I been there."

He had surgery for an ulcer in 1978 and for prostate cancer in 1995, and through it all he has remained relatively young and in good health, which he is grateful for.

"I'm a fast healer," he says. "If I cut myself, I come back in a week and you can't even see where it was at, for some reason.

"A lot of people my age done give up. I don't feel no different than when I was twenty or thirty that I can remember. . . . Matter of fact, I'm in better shape physically and mentally than I was probably at that time. I think that's one of the things that keeps you coming back over here and doing the different things we're doing. You see people ninety years old who can't get out of their chair; then you see people ninety years old driving sports cars. I want to be one of them. So far, as far as hurting and stuff, I ain't wore out."

He also hasn't tired of going from track to track and meeting up with old friends and making new ones. At each stop, he spends time with paving contractors, motorcycle dealers, lawyers, writers, governors, and homemakers.

"The King" knows that so many of these people see him as an American hero, but that's a title he is hesitant about claiming.

"I'm not special or nothing," he insists. "I was the guy who got lucky enough to do what I got to do."

In spite of an adoring public that sees him as a hero, "The King" himself insists that he is just an ordinary guy. *Dick Conway*

The memory of Richard Petty's racing days is fading, but his legend will always live on. *Dick Conway*

RICHARD'S TOP RECORDS

CAREER WINS

RANK	DRIVER	WINS
1	Richard Petty	200
2	David Pearson	105
3	Bobby Allison	85

CAREER STARTS

RANK	DRIVER	STARTS
1	Richard Petty	1184
2	Dave Marcis	883
3	Ricky Rudd	839

CAREER TOP 5 FINISHES

RANK	DRIVER	TOP 5S
1	Richard Petty	555
2	Bobby Allison	336
3	David Pearson	301

CAREER TOP 10 FINISHES

RANK	DRIVER	TOP 10S
1	Richard Petty	712
2	Bobby Allison	447
3	Dale Earnhardt	428

CAREER POLES

RANK	DRIVER	POLES
1	Richard Petty	126
2	David Pearson	113
3	Cale Yarborough	70

CAREER LAPS LED

RANK	DRIVER	LAPS LED
1	Richard Petty	52,135
2	Cale Yarborough	31,507
3	Bobby Allison	25,708

* Complete Lap Leader Records are not available for all Cup races.

CONSECUTIVE WINNING YEARS

RANK	DRIVER	YEARS
1	Richard Petty	18 (1960-1977)
2	David Pearson	17 (1964-1980)
3	Ricky Rudd	16 (1983-1998)
4	Rusty Wallace	16 (1986-2001)

CONSECUTIVE VICTORIES

RANK	DRIVER	CONSEC. WINS
1	Richard Petty	10 (1967)
2	Richard Petty	5 (1971)
3	Bobby Allison	5 (1971)

SINGLE SEASON VICTORIES

RANK	DRIVE	NO. OF WINS
1	Richard Petty	27 (1967)
2	Richard Petty	27 (1971)
3	Tim Flock	18 (1955)
4	Richard Petty	18 (1970)

SINGLE SEASON LAPS LED

RANK	DRIVER	NO. OF LAPS
1	Richard Petty	5,537 (1967)
2	Bobby Isaac	5,072 (1969)
3	Richard Petty	5,007 (1970)

APPENDIX B

RICHARD'S RACE RESULTS

GRAND NATIONAL AND WINSTON CUP CAREER BY NASCAR STATISTICIAN GREG FIELDEN

RACE NO.	RACE DATE	LOCATION	FINISH	START	CAR	LAPS	LAPS LED	STATUS	WINNINGS
1	7/18/1958	Toronto, Canada	17	7	57 Olds	55	0	Crash	$115.00
2	7/19/1958	Buffalo, NY	11	13	57 Olds	96	0	Running	$155.00
3	7/26/1958	Belmar, NJ	9		57 Olds	278	0	Running	$140.00
4	8/22/1958	Winston-Salem, NC	20	11	57 Olds	165	0	Running	$115.00
5	8/23/1958	Myrtle Beach, SC	16	9	57 Olds	166	0	Crash	$60.00
6	9/28/1958	Hillsboro, NC	31	16	57 Olds	16	0	Engine failure	$0.00
7	10/5/1958	Salisbury, NC	22		57 Olds	137	0	Running	$50.00
8	10/19/1958	North Wilkesboro, NC	23	10	57 Olds	35	0	Overheating	$50.00
9	10/26/1958	Atlanta, GA	35	35	57 Olds	29	0	Piston	$75.00
10	11/9/1958	Fayetteville, NC	13	13	57 Olds	140	0	Running	$100.00
11	2/22/1959	Daytona Beach, FL	57	6	57 Olds	8	0	Engine failure	$100.00
12	3/29/1959	Wilson, NC	3	21	57 Olds	198	0	Running	$350.00
13	3/30/1959	Winston-Salem, NC	9	12	57 Olds	195	0	Running	$150.00
14	5/3/1959	Martinsville, VA	7	25	57 Olds	490	0	Running	$375.00
15	5/17/1959	Trenton, NJ	12	11	57 Olds	95	0	Crash	$165.00
16	5/22/1959	Charlotte, NC	19	11	57 Olds	108	0	Engine failure	$50.00
17	6/14/1959	Atlanta, GA	2	27	57 Olds	150	0	Running	$1,400.00
18	6/27/1959	Winston-Salem, NC	24	3	57 Olds	14	0	Transmission	$50.00
19	7/4/1959	Daytona Beach, FL	26	4	59 Plymouth	78	0	Fuel pump	$200.00
20	7/26/1959	Charlotte, NC	12	11	57 Olds	189	0	Spindle	$110.00
21	8/1/1959	Myrtle Beach, SC	27	10	57 Olds	4	0	Ball joint	$0.00
22	8/2/1959	Charlotte, NC	20	13	57 Olds	114	0	Crash	$50.00
23	8/9/1959	Nashville, TN	29	8	59 Plymouth	12	0	Engine failure	$50.00
24	8/16/1959	Weaverville, NC	26	22	59 Plymouth	281	0	Crash	$100.00
25	9/7/1959	Darlington, SC	4	6	59 Plymouth	361	7	Running	$2,830.00
26	9/20/1959	Hillsboro, NC	3	2	59 Plymouth	100	0	Axle	$375.00
27	9/27/1959	Martinsville, VA	15	3	59 Plymouth	476	0	Running	$275.00
28	10/11/1959	Weaverville, NC	5	8	59 Plymouth	198	0	Running	$250.00
29	10/18/1959	North Wilkesboro, NC	3	5	59 Plymouth	160	0	Running	$375.00
30	10/25/1959	Concord, NC	7	11	59 Plymouth	283	0	Running	$275.00
31	11/8/1959	Charlotte, NC	12	13	59 Plymouth	174	0	Axle	$110.00
32	11/26/1959	Columbia, SC	6	6	59 Plymouth	190	0	Running	$215.00
33	2/12/1960	Daytona Beach, FL	10	5	60 Plymouth	39	0	Running	$140.00
34	2/14/1960	Daytona Beach, FL	3	19	60 Plymouth	200	29	Running	$6,450.00
35	2/28/1960	Charlotte, NC	1	7	59 Plymouth	200	18	Running	$800.00
36	3/27/1960	North Wilkesboro, NC	18	4	59 Plymouth	125	0	Engine failure	$50.00
37	4/5/1960	Columbia, SC	6	7	59 Plymouth	196	0	Running	$215.00
38	4/10/1960	Martinsville, VA	1	4	60 Plymouth	500	135	Running	$3,340.00
39	4/16/1960	Hickory, NC	3	3	60 Plymouth	249	0	Running	$375.00
40	4/17/1960	Wilson, NC	7	13	59 Plymouth	192	0	Running	$175.00
41	4/18/1960	Winston-Salem, NC	4	4	60 Plymouth	199	0	Running	$305.00
42	4/23/1960	Greenville, SC	3	3	60 Plymouth	199	0	Running	$375.00
43	4/24/1960	Weaverville, NC	9	7	60 Plymouth	127	0	Running	$140.00
44	5/14/1960	Darlington, SC	2	7	60 Plymouth	219	0	Running	$4,875.00
45	5/28/1960	Spartanburg, SC	11	11	60 Plymouth	186	0	Crash	$125.00
46	5/29/1960	Hillsboro, NC	6	1	60 Plymouth	107	0	Running	$215.00
47	6/5/1960	Richmond, VA	6	11	60 Plymouth	196	0	Running	$215.00
48	6/19/1960	Charlotte, NC	55	11	60 Plymouth	0	0	Disqualified	$0.00
49	6/26/1960	Winston-Salem, NC	4	2	60 Plymouth	197	0	Running	$250.00
50	7/4/1960	Daytona Beach, FL	11	6	60 Plymouth	96	0	Running	$600.00
51	7/10/1960	Pittsburgh, PA	2	4	60 Plymouth	185	0	Running	$525.00
52	7/17/1960	Montgomery, NY	2	2	60 Plymouth	99	0	Running	$1,600.00
53	7/23/1960	Myrtle Beach, SC	5	8	60 Plymouth	197	0	Running	$250.00
54	7/31/1960	Hampton, GA	20	12	60 Plymouth	186	0	Running	$475.00
55	8/3/1960	Birmingham, AL	2	2	60 Plymouth	198	0	Running	$535.00
56	8/7/1960	Nashville, TN	6	9	60 Plymouth	329	0	Running	$500.00
57	8/14/1960	Weaverville, NC	15	16	60 Plymouth	359	49	Crash	$250.00
58	8/16/1960	Spartanburg, SC	13	4	60 Plymouth	147	0	Battery	$100.00
59	8/18/1960	Columbia, SC	2	9	60 Plymouth	300	0	Running	$600.00
60	8/20/1960	South Boston, VA	6	3	60 Plymouth	144	0	Running	$235.00
61	8/23/1960	Winston-Salem, NC	9	3	60 Plymouth	194	0	Running	$175.00
62	9/5/1960	Darlington, SC	6	8	60 Plymouth	361	106	Running	$2,575.00
63	9/9/1960	Hickory, NC	12	8	60 Plymouth	201	0	Engine failure	$110.00
64	9/15/1960	Sumter, SC	7	4	60 Plymouth	194	0	Running	$190.00
65	9/18/1960	Hillsboro, NC	1	1	60 Plymouth	110	110	Running	$800.00
66	9/25/1960	Martinsville, VA	22	17	60 Plymouth	290	0	Crash	$75.00
67	10/2/1960	North Wilkesboro, NC	6	2	60 Plymouth	314	0	Running	$315.00
68	10/16/1960	Charlotte, NC	2	21	60 Plymouth	266	0	Running	$5,550.00
69	10/23/1960	Richmond, VA	4	5	60 Plymouth	197	0	Running	$275.00
70	10/30/1960	Hampton, GA	7	12	60 Plymouth	327	0	Running	$1,075.00
71	11/6/1960	Charlotte, NC	11	6	60 Plymouth	142	0	A-frame	$125.00
72	11/20/1960	Jacksonville, FL	4	8	60 Plymouth	197	0	Running	$275.00
73	2/24/1961	Daytona Beach, FL	16	14	61 Plymouth	37	0	Crash	$75.00
74	3/4/1961	Spartanburg, SC	2	3	60 Plymouth	199	0	Running	$525.00
75	3/5/1961	Weaverville, NC	4	10	60 Plymouth	196	0	Running	$275.00
76	3/26/1961	Hampton, GA	24	22	60 Plymouth	155	0	Engine failure	$200.00
77	4/1/1961	Greenville, SC	2	5	60 Plymouth	200	0	Running	$525.00
78	4/2/1961	Hillsboro, NC	2	4	60 Plymouth	110	0	Running	$525.00
79	4/3/1961	Winston-Salem, NC	3	6	60 Plymouth	147	0	Running	$375.00

80	4/9/1961	Martinsville, VA	8	9	61 Plymouth	146	0	Running	$175.00
81	4/16/1961	North Wilkesboro, NC	3	3	61 Plymouth	396	0	Running	$900.00
82	4/20/1961	Columbia, SC	6	7	60 Plymouth	193	0	Running	$215.00
83	4/22/1961	Hickory, NC	20	4	60 Plymouth	100	28	Radiator	$50.00
84	4/23/1961	Richmond, VA	1	1	60 Plymouth	200	182	Running	$950.00
85	4/30/1961	Martinsville, VA	23	3	61 Plymouth	243	0	Distributor	$200.00
86	5/6/1961	Darlington, SC	32	31	61 Plymouth	11	0	Engine failure	$200.00
87	5/21/1961	Charlotte, NC	1	7	61 Plymouth	67	24	Running	$800.00
88	5/28/1961	Charlotte, NC	30	1	61 Plymouth	332	47	Engine failure	$670.00
89	6/2/1961	Spartanburg, SC	15	8	60 Plymouth	70	0	Crash	$70.00
90	6/8/1961	Greenville, SC	16	8	60 Plymouth	130	0	A-frame	$60.00
91	6/10/1961	Winston-Salem, NC	5	6	60 Plymouth	198	0	Running	$250.00
92	6/23/1961	Hartsville, SC	17	10	61 Plymouth	69	0	Engine failure	$65.00
93	6/24/1961	Roanoke, VA	4	4	61 Plymouth	147	0	Running	$295.00
94	7/9/1961	Hampton, GA	3	39	61 Plymouth	164	0	Running	$2,275.00
95	7/20/1961	Columbia, SC	7	8	60 Plymouth	194	0	Running	$175.00
96	7/22/1961	Myrtle Beach, SC	17	4	61 Plymouth	43	0	Connecting rod	$50.00
97	7/29/1961	Bristol, TN	4	4	61 Plymouth	493	19	Running	$800.00
98	8/6/1961	Nashville, TN	14	2	61 Plymouth	366	362	Engine failure	$1,225.00
99	8/9/1961	Winston-Salem, NC	5	6	61 Plymouth	149	0	Running	$225.00
100	8/13/1961	Weaverville, NC	11	8	61 Plymouth	249	0	Running	$400.00
101	8/18/1961	Richmond, VA	9	4	61 Plymouth	143	0	Running	$180.00
102	8/27/1961	South Boston, VA	20	7	60 Plymouth	32	0	Engine failure	$50.00
103	9/4/1961	Darlington, SC	26	5	61 Plymouth	201	41	Engine failure	$1,110.00
104	9/8/1961	Hickory, NC	17	6	61 Plymouth	102	0	Rear end	$60.00
105	9/10/1961	Richmond, VA	18	8	61 Plymouth	157	0	Engine failure	$80.00
106	9/17/1961	Hampton, GA	5	26	61 Plymouth	264	0	Running	$1,625.00
107	9/24/1961	Martinsville, VA	17	7	61 Plymouth	319	0	Engine failure	$175.00
108	10/1/1961	North Wilkesboro, NC	3	13	61 Plymouth	316	0	Running	$850.00
109	10/15/1961	Charlotte, NC	2	22	61 Plymouth	267	0	Running	$4,870.00
110	10/22/1961	Bristol, TN	23	11	61 Plymouth	394	0	Rear end	$245.00
111	10/28/1961	Greenville, SC	4	9	61 Plymouth	195	0	Running	$275.00
112	10/29/1961	Hillsboro, NC	10	5	61 Plymouth	133	0	Transmission	$200.00
113	11/5/1961	Concord, NC	13	6	61 Plymouth	152	0	Rear end	$100.00
114	11/12/1961	Weaverville, NC	7	8	61 Plymouth	199	0	Running	$175.00
115	2/16/1962	Daytona Beach, FL	4	12	62 Plymouth	39	0	Running	$300.00
116	2/18/1962	Daytona Beach, FL	2	10	62 Plymouth	200	32	Running	$10,250.00
117	2/25/1962	Concord, NC	2		62 Plymouth	78	0	Running	$300.00
118	3/4/1962	Weaverville, NC	8	7	62 Plymouth	190	0	Running	$175.00
119	3/17/1962	Savannah, GA	14	8	62 Plymouth	52	0	Running	$100.00
120	3/18/1962	Hillsboro, NC	2	2	62 Plymouth	110	26	Running	$600.00
121	4/1/1962	Richmond, VA	20	3	61 Plymouth	34	34	Radiator	$75.00
122	4/13/1962	Columbia, SC	7	6	61 Plymouth	197	0	Running	$200.00
123	4/15/1962	North Wilkesboro, NC	1	15	62 Plymouth	400	142	Running	$2,725.00
124	4/19/1962	Greenville, SC	11	2	62 Plymouth	139	0	Ball joint	$230.00
125	4/21/1962	Myrtle Beach, SC	2	7	60 Plymouth	198	0	Running	$600.00
126	4/22/1962	Martinsville, VA	1	7	62 Plymouth	500	145	Running	$3,400.00
127	4/23/1962	Winston-Salem, NC	5	6	61 Plymouth	107	0	Running	$225.00
128	4/29/1962	Bristol, TN	16	11	62 Plymouth	368	9	Engine failure	$300.00
129	5/4/1962	Richmond, VA	3	7	60 Plymouth	199	0	Running	$375.00
130	5/5/1962	Hickory, NC	6	4	62 Plymouth	234	0	Running	$240.00
131	5/6/1962	Concord, NC	9	1	62 Plymouth	134	134	Axle	$150.00
132	5/12/1962	Darlington, SC	15	7	62 Plymouth	201	0	Running	$500.00
133	5/19/1962	Spartanburg, SC	3	7	60 Plymouth	200	0	Running	$400.00
134	5/27/1962	Charlotte, NC	4	21	62 Plymouth	397	5	Running	$5,400.00
135	6/10/1962	Hampton, GA	23	27	62 Plymouth	207	0	Running	$250.00
136	6/16/1962	Winston-Salem, NC	3	4	62 Plymouth	196	0	Running	$375.00
137	6/19/1962	Augusta, GA	3	5	62 Plymouth	198	0	Running	$400.00
138	6/22/1962	Richmond, VA	19	2	62 Plymouth	111	0	Rear end	$75.00
139	6/23/1962	South Boston, VA	3	5	62 Plymouth	267	0	Running	$400.00
140	7/4/1962	Daytona Beach, FL	30	11	62 Plymouth	6	0	Crash	$275.00
141	7/7/1962	Columbia, SC	20	2	62 Plymouth	20	0	Engine failure	$50.00
142	7/13/1962	Asheville, NC	3	2	62 Plymouth	248	0	Running	$400.00
143	7/14/1962	Greenville, SC	1	4	62 Plymouth	200	1	Running	$1,000.00
144	7/17/1962	Augusta, GA	2	3	62 Plymouth	200	0	Running	$600.00
145	7/20/1962	Savannah, GA	3	9	62 Plymouth	200	0	Running	$400.00
146	7/21/1962	Myrtle Beach, SC	16	5	62 Plymouth	130	0	Idler arm	$75.00
147	7/29/1962	Bristol, TN	3	16	62 Plymouth	500	47	Running	$1,540.00
148	8/3/1962	Chattanooga, TN	4	1	62 Plymouth	197	172	Running	$300.00
149	8/5/1962	Nashville, TN	2	2	62 Plymouth	495	135	Running	$1,875.00
150	8/8/1962	Huntsville, AL	1	1	62 Plymouth	200	200	Running	$580.00
151	8/12/1962	Weaverville, NC	7	6	62 Plymouth	485	0	Running	$600.00
152	8/15/1962	Roanoke, VA	1	2	62 Plymouth	200	1	Running	$550.00
153	8/18/1962	Winston-Salem, NC	1	3	62 Plymouth	200	54	Running	$600.00
154	8/21/1962	Spartanburg, SC	1	1	62 Plymouth	200	1	Running	$1,000.00
155	8/25/1962	Valdosta, GA	2	1	62 Plymouth	199	0	Running	$600.00
156	9/3/1962	Darlington, SC	5	6	62 Plymouth	363	95	Running	$5,450.00
157	9/7/1962	Hickory, NC	10	5	62 Plymouth	220	0	Running	$140.00
158	9/9/1962	Richmond, VA	4	9	62 Plymouth	296	0	Running	$675.00
159	9/11/1962	Moycock, NC	11	4	62 Plymouth	151	0	Axle	$155.00
160	9/13/1962	Augusta, GA	2	5	62 Plymouth	200	0	Running	$600.00
161	9/23/1962	Martinsville, VA	2	13	62 Plymouth	497	0	Running	$1,650.00
162	9/30/1962	North Wilkesboro, NC	1	5	62 Plymouth	320	160	Running	$2,560.00
163	10/14/1962	Charlotte, NC	16	12	62 Plymouth	250	0	Running	$475.00
164	10/28/1962	Hampton, GA	4	15	62 Plymouth	266	3	Running	$2,415.00
165	11/4/1962	Birmingham, AL	2	6	62 Plymouth	199	8	Running	$600.00
166	11/11/1962	Tampa, FL	1	5	62 Plymouth	200	158	Running	$780.00
167	11/22/1962	Randleman, NC	11	5	62 Plymouth	188	0	Transmission	$145.00
168	1/20/1963	Riverside, CA	41	15	63 Plymouth	27	0	Transmission	$300.00
169	2/22/1963	Daytona Beach, FL	12	22	63 Plymouth	38	0	Running	$125.00
170	2/24/1963	Daytona Beach, FL	6	23	63 Plymouth	198	0	Running	$2,500.00
171	3/2/1963	Spartanburg, SC	1	2	63 Plymouth	200	2	Running	$1,000.00
172	3/3/1963	Weaverville, NC	1	3	63 Plymouth	200	52	Running	$1,000.00

173	3/10/1963	Hillsboro, NC	3	3	63 Plymouth	165	15	Running	$750.00
174	3/17/1963	Hampton, GA	8	8	62 Plymouth	328	0	Running	$1,000.00
175	3/24/1963	Hickory, NC	2	3	63 Plymouth	249	84	Running	$700.00
176	3/31/1963	Bristol, TN	4	16	63 Plymouth	495	0	Running	$1,225.00
177	4/4/1963	Augusta, GA	2	2	62 Plymouth	112	0	Running	$600.00
178	4/7/1963	Richmond, VA	6	11	63 Plymouth	240	0	Running	$375.00
179	4/13/1963	Greenville, SC	4	3	62 Plymouth	199	44	Running	$300.00
180	4/14/1963	South Boston, VA	1	2	63 Plymouth	400	325	Running	$1,500.00
181	4/15/1963	Winston-Salem, NC	11	1	63 Plymouth	146	146	Fuel pump	$130.00
182	4/21/1963	Martinsville, VA	1	8	63 Plymouth	500	41	Running	$3,375.00
183	4/28/1963	North Wilkesboro, NC	1	7	63 Plymouth	257	130	Running	$3,575.00
184	5/2/1963	Columbia, SC	1	1	63 Plymouth	200	1	Running	$1,000.00
185	5/5/1963	Randleman, NC	13	2	63 Plymouth	171	0	Running	$160.00
186	5/11/1963	Darlington, SC	3	9	63 Plymouth	219	101	Running	$4,980.00
187	5/18/1963	Manassas, VA	1	1	63 Plymouth	300	292	Running	$1,000.00
188	5/19/1963	Richmond, VA	2	2	63 Plymouth	298	107	Running	$600.00
189	6/2/1963	Charlotte, NC	36	18	63 Plymouth	90	0	Camshaft	$450.00
190	6/9/1963	Birmingham, AL	1	2	63 Plymouth	200	178	Running	$1,000.00
191	6/30/1963	Hampton, GA	12	14	63 Plymouth	262	0	Running	$600.00
192	7/4/1963	Daytona Beach, FL	8	18	63 Plymouth	154	0	Running	$1,250.00
193	7/7/1963	Myrtle Beach, SC	15	1	63 Plymouth	60	30	Crash	$100.00
194	7/10/1963	Savannah, GA	15	1	63 Plymouth	38	6	Crash	$85.00
195	7/11/1963	Moyock, NC	11	4	63 Plymouth	145	0	Differential	$145.00
196	7/13/1963	Winston-Salem, NC	8	3	63 Plymouth	193	0	Running	$180.00
197	7/14/1963	Asheville, NC	2	3	63 Plymouth	300	120	Running	$600.00
198	7/19/1963	Old Bridge, NJ	16	4	63 Plymouth	83	0	Brakes	$75.00
199	7/21/1963	Bridgehampton, NY	1	1	63 Plymouth	35	33	Running	$1,000.00
200	7/28/1963	Bristol, TN	2	15	63 Plymouth	500	3	Running	$2,365.00
201	7/30/1963	Greenville, SC	1	7	63 Plymouth	200	52	Running	$1,000.00
202	8/4/1963	Nashville, TN	4	1	63 Plymouth	348	96	Running	$675.00
203	8/8/1963	Columbia, SC	1	1	63 Plymouth	200	138	Running	$1,140.00
204	8/11/1963	Weaverville, NC	2	10	63 Plymouth	499	35	Running	$1,425.00
205	8/14/1963	Spartanburg, SC	2	3	63 Plymouth	200	1	Running	$600.00
206	8/16/1963	Winston-Salem, NC	2	3	63 Plymouth	199	0	Running	$500.00
207	8/18/1963	Huntington, WV	10	3	63 Plymouth	286	53	Running	$250.00
208	9/2/1963	Darlington, SC	12	18	63 Plymouth	341	0	Running	$1,030.00
209	9/6/1963	Hickory, NC	15	5	63 Plymouth	196	0	Oil line	$95.00
210	9/8/1963	Richmond, VA	6	3	63 Plymouth	286	0	Distributor	$425.00
211	9/22/1963	Martinsville, VA	5	9	63 Plymouth	496	0	Running	$775.00
212	9/24/1963	Moyock, NC	4	5	63 Plymouth	290	0	Running	$300.00
213	9/29/1963	North Wilkesboro, NC	26	3	63 Plymouth	45	0	Engine failure	$125.00
214	10/5/1963	Randleman, NC	1	2	63 Plymouth	200	41	Running	$580.00
215	10/13/1963	Charlotte, NC	6	15	63 Plymouth	257	0	Running	$1,200.00
216	10/20/1963	South Boston, VA	1	4	63 Plymouth	400	187	Running	$1,550.00
217	10/27/1963	Hillsboro, NC	6	5	63 Plymouth	146	34	Running	$325.00
218	11/3/1963	Riverside, CA	36	11	63 Plymouth	5	0	Transmission	$400.00
219	11/10/1963	Concord, NC	3	4	63 Plymouth	248	13	Running	$650.00
220	11/17/1963	Augusta, GA	19	15	63 Plymouth	94	56	Pinion G	$820.00
221	12/1/1963	Jacksonville, FL	5	2	63 Plymouth	193	103	Running	$275.00
222	12/29/1963	Savannah, GA	1	5	63 Plymouth	200	133	Running	$1,000.00
223	1/19/1964	Riverside, CA	26	2	63 Plymouth	101	27	Transmission	$940.00
224	2/21/1964	Daytona Beach, FL	3	1	64 Plymouth	40	39	Running	$400.00
225	2/23/1964	Daytona Beach, FL	1	2	64 Plymouth	200	184	Running	$33,300.00
226	3/8/1964	Richmond, VA	2	6	64 Plymouth	250	29	Running	$1,000.00
227	3/22/1964	Bristol, TN	8	4	64 Plymouth	489	0	Running	$675.00
228	3/28/1964	Greenville, SC	16	7	64 Plymouth	87	27	Rear end	$100.00
229	3/30/1964	Winston-Salem, NC	3	3	64 Plymouth	199	0	Running	$425.00
230	4/5/1964	Hampton, GA	7	8	64 Plymouth	325	0	Running	$1,100.00
231	4/11/1964	Weaverville, NC	17	4	64 Plymouth	146	0	Rear end	$100.00
232	4/12/1964	Hillsboro, NC	12	2	64 Plymouth	117	51	Clutch	$100.00
233	4/14/1964	Spartanburg, SC	15	3	64 Plymouth	83	0	Rear end	$100.00
234	4/16/1964	Columbia, SC	15	3	64 Plymouth	129	0	Rear end	$100.00
235	4/19/1964	North Wilkesboro, NC	7	2	64 Plymouth	392	4	Running	$550.00
236	4/26/1964	Martinsville, VA	6	6	64 Plymouth	490	0	Running	$675.00
237	5/1/1964	Savannah, GA	3	2	64 Plymouth	197	0	Running	$400.00
238	5/9/1964	Darlington, SC	10	2	64 Plymouth	211	95	Running	$840.00
239	5/15/1964	Hampton, VA	17	15	64 Plymouth	1	0	Engine failure	$100.00
240	5/16/1964	Hickory, NC	3	9	64 Plymouth	249	0	Running	$400.00
241	5/17/1964	South Boston, VA	1	7	63 Plymouth	267	181	Running	$1,000.00
242	5/24/1964	Charlotte, NC	2	5	64 Plymouth	396	0	Running	$10,455.00
243	5/30/1964	Greenville, SC	2	4	63 Plymouth	199	0	Running	$600.00
244	5/31/1964	Asheville, NC	2	1	64 Plymouth	298	129	Running	$600.00
245	6/7/1964	Hampton, GA	2	13	64 Plymouth	267	42	Running	$5,790.00
246	6/11/1964	Concord, NC	1	1	64 Plymouth	200	90	Running	$1,000.00
247	6/14/1964	Nashville, TN	1	2	64 Plymouth	200	127	Running	$1,000.00
248	6/19/1964	Chattanooga, TN	2	1	64 Plymouth	298	60	Running	$600.00
249	6/21/1964	Birmingham, AL	2	4	64 Plymouth	199	0	Running	$600.00
250	6/23/1964	Valdosta, GA	13	11	64 Plymouth	179	0	Running	$110.00
251	6/26/1964	Spartanburg, SC	1	2	64 Plymouth	200	58	Running	$1,000.00
252	7/4/1964	Daytona Beach, FL	16	3	64 Plymouth	103	102	Engine failure	$1,400.00
253	7/8/1964	Manassas, VA	8	2	64 Plymouth	366	0	Differential	$225.00
254	7/10/1964	Old Bridge, NJ	3	3	64 Plymouth	198	55	Running	$400.00
255	7/12/1964	Bridgehampton, NY	13	1	64 Plymouth	21	1	Engine failure	$385.00
256	7/15/1964	Islip, NY	3	3	64 Plymouth	295	0	Running	$400.00
257	7/19/1964	Watkins Glen, NY	21	4	64 Plymouth	10	0	Crash	$150.00
258	7/21/1964	New Oxford, PA	2	3	64 Plymouth	200	0	Running	$600.00
259	7/26/1964	Bristol, TN	2	1	64 Plymouth	499	442	Rear end	$2,730.00
260	8/2/1964	Nashville, TN	1	1	64 Plymouth	400	400	Running	$2,150.00
261	8/7/1964	Myrtle Beach, SC	2	2	64 Plymouth	199	0	Running	$600.00
262	8/9/1964	Weaverville, NC	25	6	64 Plymouth	140	0	Crash	$250.00
263	8/13/1964	Moyock, NC	3	2	64 Plymouth	296	0	Running	$400.00
264	8/16/1964	Huntington, WV	1	3	64 Plymouth	500	396	Running	$2,550.00
265	8/21/1964	Columbia, SC	17	2	64 Plymouth	17	17	Oil pressure	$100.00

266	8/22/1964	Winston-Salem, NC	2	2	64 Plymouth	249	0	Running	$600.00
267	8/23/1964	Roanoke, VA	15	6	64 Plymouth	148	0	Engine failure	$125.00
268	9/7/1964	Darlington, SC	3	1	64 Plymouth	360	252	Running	$8,170.00
269	9/11/1964	Hickory, NC	5	2	64 Plymouth	238	0	Running	$275.00
270	9/14/1964	Richmond, VA	3	10	64 Plymouth	292	0	Running	$1,200.00
271	9/18/1964	Manassas, VA	3	2	64 Plymouth	496	20	Running	$725.00
272	9/20/1964	Hillsboro, NC	16	4	64 Plymouth	111	7	Overheating	$100.00
273	9/27/1964	Martinsville, VA	2	21	64 Plymouth	500	5	Running	$1,725.00
274	10/9/1964	Savannah, GA	2	3	64 Plymouth	199	0	Running	$600.00
275	10/11/1964	North Wilkesboro, NC	19	3	64 Plymouth	153	0	Rear end	$250.00
276	10/18/1964	Charlotte, NC	3	1	64 Plymouth	265	188	Crash	$4,245.00
277	10/25/1964	Harris, NC	1	4	64 Plymouth	334	175	Running	$1,000.00
278	11/1/1964	Augusta, GA	25	2	64 Plymouth	109	0	Crash	$50.00
279	11/8/1964	Jacksonville, NC	2	4	64 Plymouth	199	26	Running	$600.00
280	7/25/1965	Bristol, TN	17	2	64 Plymouth	338	0	Differential	$560.00
281	7/31/1965	Nashville, TN	1	1	65 Plymouth	400	335	Running	$2,350.00
282	8/5/1965	Shelby, NC	2	4	64 Plymouth	196	0	Running	$600.00
283	8/8/1965	Weaverville, NC	1	1	65 Plymouth	500	346	Running	$3,200.00
284	8/13/1965	Maryville, TN	3	2	64 Plymouth	195	0	Running	$400.00
285	8/19/1965	Columbia, SC	2	5	65 Plymouth	200	0	Running	$800.00
286	8/24/1965	Moyock, NC	3	1	65 Plymouth	300	31	Running	$600.00
287	8/28/1965	Winston-Salem, NC	2	1	65 Plymouth	246	1	Running	$800.00
288	9/10/1965	Hickory, NC	1	5	65 Plymouth	250	40	Running	$1,200.00
289	9/14/1965	New Oxford, PA	19	1	65 Plymouth	101	0	Suspension	$300.00
290	9/17/1965	Manassas, VA	1	2	65 Plymouth	400	319	Running	$1,300.00
291	9/26/1965	Martinsville, VA	2	1	65 Plymouth	499	19	Running	$2,400.00
292	10/3/1965	North Wilkesboro, NC	33	2	65 Plymouth	14	0	Crash	$450.00
293	10/31/1965	Rockingham, NC	36	1	65 Plymouth	58	0	Crash	$1,240.00
294	11/14/1965	Augusta, GA	1	1	65 Plymouth	300	132	Running	$1,700.00
295	1/23/1966	Riverside, CA	25	7	65 Plymouth	105	0	Engine failure	$550.00
296	2/25/1966	Daytona Beach, FL	2	1	66 Plymouth	40	25	Running	$600.00
297	2/27/1966	Daytona Beach, FL	1	1	66 Plymouth	198	108	Running	$28,150.00
298	3/27/1966	Hampton, GA	25	1	66 Plymouth	185	131	Engine failure	$1,530.00
299	4/3/1966	Hickory, NC	10	16	65 Plymouth	236	7	Running	$140.00
300	4/7/1966	Columbia, SC	6	18	65 Plymouth	195	0	Running	$240.00
301	4/9/1966	Greenville, SC	2	9	65 Plymouth	199	0	Running	$600.00
302	4/11/1966	Winston-Salem, NC	3	5	65 Plymouth	198	0	Running	$425.00
303	4/17/1966	North Wilkesboro, NC	11	4	65 Plymouth	347	92	Running	$400.00
304	4/24/1966	Martinsville, VA	3	4	66 Plymouth	495	0	Running	$1,250.00
305	4/30/1966	Darlington, SC	1	1	66 Plymouth	291	271	Running	$12,115.00
306	5/7/1966	Hampton, VA	1	1	66 Plymouth	250	177	Running	$1,000.00
307	5/10/1966	Macon, GA	1	1	66 Plymouth	200	159	Running	$1,000.00
308	5/15/1966	Richmond, VA	2	10	66 Plymouth	248	9	Running	$1,250.00
309	5/22/1966	Charlotte, NC	22	1	66 Plymouth	236	6	Engine failure	$1,320.00
310	5/29/1966	Moyock, NC	18	1	65 Plymouth	84	84	Ignition	$100.00
311	6/2/1966	Asheville, NC	17	1	65 Plymouth	89	9	Crash	$100.00
312	6/12/1966	Weaverville, NC	1	1	66 Plymouth	300	176	Running	$1,400.00
313	6/15/1966	Beltsville, MD	21	1	66 Plymouth	71	71	Engine failure	$100.00
314	7/4/1966	Daytona Beach, FL	29	2	64 Plymouth	86	0	Crash	$530.00
315	7/12/1966	Oxford, ME	3	2	66 Plymouth	299	0	Running	$450.00
316	7/14/1966	Fonda, NY	2	1	66 Plymouth	200	23	Running	$675.00
317	7/16/1966	Islip, NY	15	8	66 Plymouth	202	0	W Bearing	$100.00
318	7/24/1966	Bristol, TN	2	3	66 Plymouth	500	336	Running	$2,950.00
319	7/28/1966	Maryville, TN	29	7	66 Plymouth	17	0	Steering	$0.00
320	7/30/1966	Nashville, TN	1	1	66 Plymouth	400	400	Running	$2,750.00
321	8/7/1966	Hampton, GA	1	5	66 Plymouth	267	90	Running	$13,525.00
322	8/18/1966	Columbia, SC	2	3	66 Plymouth	200	2	Running	$600.00
323	8/21/1966	Weaverville, NC	18	4	66 Plymouth	369	125	Heating	$200.00
324	8/24/1966	Beltsville, MD	20	2	66 Plymouth	30	30	Engine failure	$100.00
325	8/27/1966	Winston-Salem, NC	2	1	66 Plymouth	250	113	Running	$600.00
326	9/5/1966	Darlington, SC	2	2	66 Plymouth	364	131	Running	$8,975.00
327	9/9/1966	Hickory, NC	2	1	66 Plymouth	249	0	Running	$600.00
328	9/11/1966	Richmond, VA	12	3	66 Plymouth	220	27	Differential	$225.00
329	9/25/1966	Martinsville, VA	23	3	66 Plymouth	263	0	Ignition	$375.00
330	10/2/1966	North Wilkesboro, NC	26	2	66 Plymouth	186	0	Ignition	$275.00
331	10/16/1966	Charlotte, NC	38	4	66 Plymouth	48	0	Suspension	$580.00
332	10/30/1966	Rockingham, NC	28	2	66 Plymouth	320	180	Engine failure	$650.00
333	11/13/1966	Augusta, GA	1	3	66 Plymouth	300	223	Running	$1,735.00
334	1/29/1967	Riverside, CA	21	4	66 Plymouth	103	5	Radiator	$680.00
335	2/24/1967	Daytona Beach, FL	5	1	67 Plymouth	40	2	Running	$300.00
336	2/26/1967	Daytona Beach, FL	8	2	67 Plymouth	193	0	Engine failure	$3,750.00
337	3/5/1967	Weaverville, NC	1	2	67 Plymouth	300	150	Running	$1,800.00
338	3/19/1967	Bristol, TN	34	3	67 Plymouth	6	4	Crash	$225.00
339	3/25/1967	Greenville, SC	19	6	67 Plymouth	95	2	Crash	$100.00
340	3/27/1967	Winston-Salem, NC	2	2	67 Plymouth	198	91	Running	$550.00
341	4/2/1967	Hampton, GA	22	2	67 Plymouth	215	17	Engine failure	$710.00
342	4/6/1967	Columbia, SC	1	2	67 Plymouth	200	169	Running	$1,000.00
343	4/9/1967	Hickory, NC	1	1	67 Plymouth	250	83	Running	$1,000.00
344	4/16/1967	North Wilkesboro, NC	7	2	67 Plymouth	389	0	Running	$500.00
345	4/23/1967	Martinsville, VA	1	2	67 Plymouth	500	118	Running	$4,450.00
346	4/28/1967	Savannah, GA	2	2	67 Plymouth	200	66	Running	$600.00
347	4/30/1967	Richmond, VA	1	1	67 Plymouth	250	141	Running	$2,150.00
348	5/13/1967	Darlington, SC	1	2	67 Plymouth	291	266	Running	$14,090.00
349	5/19/1967	Beltsville, MD	2	1	67 Plymouth	200	151	Running	$600.00
350	5/20/1967	Hampton, VA	1	1	67 Plymouth	250	223	Running	$1,000.00
351	5/28/1967	Charlotte, NC	4	5	67 Plymouth	397	0	Running	$4,875.00
352	6/2/1967	Asheville, NC	3	1	67 Plymouth	298	21	Running	$400.00
353	6/6/1967	Macon, GA	1	1	67 Plymouth	300	242	Running	$1,400.00
354	6/8/1967	Maryville, TN	1	6	67 Plymouth	200	121	Running	$1,000.00
355	6/10/1967	Birmingham, AL	3	2	67 Plymouth	160	0	Running	$400.00
356	6/18/1967	Rockingham, NC	1	2	67 Plymouth	500	249	Running	$16,175.00
357	6/24/1967	Greenville, SC	1	1	67 Plymouth	200	192	Running	$1,000.00
358	6/27/1967	Montgomery, AL	2	1	67 Plymouth	200	60	Running	$600.00

359	7/4/1967	Daytona Beach, FL	11	3	67 Plymouth	153	0	Running	$750.00
360	7/9/1967	Trenton, NJ	1	1	67 Plymouth	300	244	Running	$4,350.00
361	7/11/1967	Oxford, ME	2	4	67 Plymouth	299	1	Running	$700.00
362	7/13/1967	Fonda, NY	1	1	67 Plymouth	200	118	Running	$1,150.00
363	7/15/1967	Islip, NY	1	1	67 Plymouth	300	66	Running	$1,150.00
364	7/23/1967	Bristol, TN	1	1	67 Plymouth	500	225	Running	$6,050.00
365	7/27/1967	Maryville, TN	2	7	67 Plymouth	200	0	Running	$600.00
366	7/29/1967	Nashville, TN	1	2	67 Plymouth	400	155	Running	$2,050.00
367	8/6/1967	Hampton, GA	17	2	67 Plymouth	262	127	Engine failure	$1,485.00
368	8/12/1967	Winston-Salem, NC	1	1	67 Plymouth	250	250	Running	$100.00
369	8/17/1967	Columbia, SC	1	1	67 Plymouth	200	29	Running	$1,000.00
370	8/25/1967	Savannah, GA	1	1	67 Plymouth	200	200	Running	$1,000.00
371	9/4/1967	Darlington, SC	1	1	67 Plymouth	364	345	Running	$26,900.00
372	9/8/1967	Hickory, NC	1	2	67 Plymouth	250	70	Running	$1,500.00
373	9/10/1967	Richmond, VA	1	2	67 Plymouth	300	183	Running	$2,450.00
374	9/15/1967	Beltsville, MD	1	1	67 Plymouth	300	171	Running	$1,400.00
375	9/17/1967	Hillsboro, NC	1	1	67 Plymouth	167	88	Running	$1,500.00
376	9/24/1967	Martinsville, VA	1	5	66 Plymouth	500	195	Running	$4,400.00
377	10/1/1967	North Wilkesboro, NC	1	5	67 Plymouth	400	256	Running	$4,725.00
378	10/15/1967	Charlotte, NC	18	5	67 Plymouth	268	0	Engine failure	$1,225.00
379	10/29/1967	Rockingham, NC	28	5	67 Plymouth	191	73	Crash	$600.00
380	11/5/1967	Weaverville, NC	2	6	67 Plymouth	500	95	Running	$2,300.00
381	11/12/1967	Macon, GA	2	6	67 Plymouth	499	0	Running	$2,040.00
382	11/26/1967	Montgomery, AL	1	1	67 Plymouth	200	154	Running	$1,200.00
383	1/21/1968	Riverside, CA	10	4	67 Plymouth	163	0	Engine failure	$1,650.00
384	2/25/1968	Daytona Beach, FL	8	2	68 Plymouth	198	4	Running	$4,350.00
385	3/17/1968	Bristol, TN	2	1	68 Plymouth	500	108	Running	$4,125.00
386	3/24/1968	Richmond, VA	17	3	68 Plymouth	137	48	Engine failure	$325.00
387	3/31/1968	Hampton, GA	6	12	68 Plymouth	331	0	Running	$1,775.00
388	4/7/1968	Hickory, NC	1	4	67 Plymouth	250	75	Running	$1,200.00
389	4/13/1968	Greenville, SC	1	3	68 Plymouth	200	53	Running	$1,200.00
390	4/18/1968	Columbia, SC	5	1	68 Plymouth	198	14	Running	$475.00
391	4/21/1968	North Wilkesboro, NC	26	6	68 Plymouth	210	39	Engine failure	$500.00
392	4/28/1968	Martinsville, VA	15	2	68 Plymouth	449	284	Rear end	$1,004.00
393	5/3/1968	Augusta, GA	18	4	68 Plymouth	86	0	Axle	$300.00
394	5/5/1968	Weaverville, NC	3	2	68 Plymouth	297	0	Running	$900.00
395	5/11/1968	Darlington, SC	3	11	68 Plymouth	291	21	Running	$5,330.00
396	5/17/1968	Beltsville, MD	14	1	68 Plymouth	158	158	Engine failure	$300.00
397	5/18/1968	Hampton, VA	6	1	68 Plymouth	242	106	Engine failure	$440.00
398	5/26/1968	Charlotte, NC	38	6	68 Plymouth	186	1	Ignition	$1,705.00
399	5/31/1968	Asheville, NC	1	1	68 Plymouth	300	300	Running	$1,200.00
400	6/2/1968	Macon, GA	3	4	68 Plymouth	300	54	Running	$900.00
401	6/6/1968	Maryville, TN	1	4	68 Plymouth	200	101	Running	$1,200.00
402	6/8/1968	Birmingham, AL	1	2	68 Plymouth	160	159	Running	$1,200.00
403	6/16/1968	Rockingham, NC	26	3	68 Plymouth	236	0	Oil pressure	$1,115.00
404	6/22/1968	Greenville, SC	1	2	68 Plymouth	200	31	Running	$1,200.00
405	7/4/1968	Daytona Beach, FL	21	2	68 Plymouth	132	5	Engine failure	$1,395.00
406	7/7/1968	Islip, NY	4	3	68 Plymouth	298	97	Running	$500.00
407	7/9/1968	Oxford, ME	1	2	68 Plymouth	300	187	Running	$1,350.00
408	7/11/1968	Fonda, NY	1	2	68 Plymouth	200	180	Running	$1,200.00
409	7/14/1968	Trenton, NJ	22	5	68 Plymouth	162	12	Engine failure	$625.00
410	7/21/1968	Bristol, TN	24	8	68 Plymouth	236	0	Fan belt	$800.00
411	7/25/1968	Maryville, TN	1	2	68 Plymouth	200	161	Running	$1,200.00
412	7/27/1968	Nashville, TN	2	1	68 Plymouth	298	231	Running	$1,700.00
413	8/4/1968	Hampton, GA	5	10	68 Plymouth	333	7	Running	$2,535.00
414	8/8/1968	Columbia, SC	21	2	68 Plymouth	72	0	Oil pan	$300.00
415	8/10/1968	Winston-Salem, NC	2	1	68 Plymouth	250	139	Running	$850.00
416	8/18/1968	Weaverville, NC	26	3	68 Plymouth	52	0	A-frame	$425.00
417	8/23/1968	South Boston, VA	1	1	68 Plymouth	267	265	Running	$1,200.00
418	8/24/1968	Hampton, VA	2	3	68 Plymouth	250	0	Running	$800.00
419	9/2/1968	Darlington, SC	20	6	68 Plymouth	273	7	Engine failure	$1,450.00
420	9/6/1968	Hickory, NC	4	1	68 Plymouth	244	13	Running	$500.00
421	9/8/1968	Richmond, VA	1	1	68 Plymouth	300	215	Running	$2,400.00
422	9/13/1968	Beltsville, MD	3	2	68 Plymouth	294	0	Running	$700.00
423	9/15/1968	Hillsboro, NC	1	1	68 Plymouth	167	155	Running	$1,600.00
424	9/22/1968	Martinsville, VA	1	6	68 Plymouth	500	324	Running	$5,999.00
425	9/29/1968	North Wilkesboro, NC	1	3	68 Plymouth	400	315	Running	$5,975.00
426	10/5/1968	Augusta, GA	3	2	68 Plymouth	200	0	Running	$600.00
427	10/20/1968	Charlotte, NC	32	6	68 Plymouth	135	0	Engine failure	$1,450.00
28	10/27/1968	Rockingham, NC	1	4	68 Plymouth	500	216	Running	$17,075.00
429	11/3/1968	Jefferson, GA	2	7	68 Plymouth	200	0	Running	$800.00
430	11/17/1968	Macon, GA	1	5	68 Plymouth	500	362	Running	$3,500.00
431	12/8/1968	Montgomery, AL	2	1	68 Plymouth	200	125	Running	$600.00
432	2/1/1969	Riverside, CA	1	4	69 Ford	186	103	Running	$19,650.00
433	2/20/1969	Daytona Beach, FL	6	10	69 Ford	49	2	Running	$400.00
434	2/23/1969	Daytona Beach, FL	8	12	69 Ford	196	0	Running	$3,150.00
435	3/9/1969	Rockingham, NC	5	5	69 Ford	492	0	Running	$1,850.00
436	3/16/1969	Augusta, GA	2	2	69 Ford	200	0	Running	$600.00
437	3/23/1969	Bristol, TN	7	9	69 Ford	484	0	Running	$575.00
438	3/30/1969	Hampton, GA	9	7	69 Ford	312	0	Engine failure	$1,700.00
439	4/3/1969	Columbia, SC	3	4	69 Ford	199	84	Running	$400.00
440	4/6/1969	Hickory, NC	2	5	69 Ford	248	0	Running	$1,300.00
441	4/8/1969	Greenville, SC	5	4	69 Ford	197	17	Running	$325.00
442	4/13/1969	Richmond, VA	2	3	69 Ford	499	21	Running	$1,800.00
443	4/20/1969	North Wilkesboro, NC	7	4	69 Ford	388	0	Engine failure	$600.00
444	4/27/1969	Martinsville, VA	1	6	69 Ford	500	65	Running	$10,275.00
445	5/4/1969	Weaverville, NC	23	3	69 Ford	52	0	Crash	$330.00
446	5/10/1969	Darlington, SC	11	2	69 Ford	263	48	Drive shaft	$1,050.00
447	5/25/1969	Charlotte, NC	19	5	69 Ford	336	95	Engine failure	$1,675.00
448	6/1/1969	Macon, GA	3	3	69 Ford	299	0	Running	$1,000.00
449	6/5/1969	Maryville, TN	20	2	69 Ford	60	0	Crash	$270.00
450	6/15/1969	Brooklyn, MI	3	5	69 Ford	250	0	Running	$5,875.00
451	6/19/1969	Kingsport, TN	1	3	69 Ford	250	41	Running	$1,000.00

452	6/21/1969	Greenville, SC	3	2	69 Ford	200	0	Running	$400.00
453	6/26/1969	Raleigh, NC	2	4	69 Ford	197	18	Running	$600.00
454	7/4/1969	Daytona Beach, FL	5	4	69 Ford	156	4	Running	$1,950.00
455	7/6/1969	Dover, DE	1	3	69 Ford	300	150	Running	$4,725.00
456	7/10/1969	Thompson, CT	25	2	69 Ford	96	96	Rear end	$250.00
457	7/13/1969	Trenton, NJ	29	3	69 Ford	36	0	Engine failure	$325.00
458	7/15/1969	Beltsville, MD	1	1	69 Ford	300	91	Running	$2,500.00
459	7/20/1969	Bristol, TN	23	2	69 Ford	60	0	Engine failure	$440.00
460	7/26/1969	Nashville, TN	1	1	69 Ford	400	398	Running	$3,000.00
461	7/27/1969	Maryville, TN	1	3	69 Ford	200	127	Running	$1,000.00
462	8/10/1969	Hampton, GA	3	3	69 Ford	334	26	Running	$6,100.00
463	8/17/1969	Brooklyn, MI	3	5	69 Ford	165	12	Running	$7,020.00
464	8/21/1969	South Boston, VA	3	2	69 Ford	266	3	Running	$400.00
465	8/22/1969	Winston-Salem, NC	1	1	69 Ford	250	109	Running	$1,000.00
466	8/24/1969	Weaverville, NC	23	2	69 Ford	120	43	Crash	$440.00
467	9/1/1969	Darlington, SC	9	6	69 Ford	220	0	Running	$1,600.00
468	9/5/1969	Hickory, NC	3	2	69 Ford	247	66	Running	$900.00
469	9/7/1969	Richmond, VA	19	1	69 Ford	171	164	Rear end	$580.00
470	9/18/1969	Columbia, SC	2	1	69 Ford	200	131	Running	$600.00
471	9/28/1969	Martinsville, VA	1	6	69 Ford	500	36	Running	$10,085.00
472	10/5/1969	North Wilkesboro, NC	2	3	69 Ford	400	270	Running	$3,000.00
473	10/12/1969	Charlotte, NC	27	2	69 Ford	239	7	Engine failure	$1,260.00
474	10/17/1969	Savannah, GA	2	3	69 Ford	200	0	Running	$600.00
475	10/19/1969	Augusta, GA	2	3	69 Ford	200	2	Running	$600.00
476	10/26/1969	Rockingham, NC	32	7	69 Ford	113	6	Crash	$680.00
477	11/2/1969	Jefferson, GA	3	3	69 Ford	198	0	Running	$500.00
478	11/9/1969	Macon, GA	6	4	69 Ford	469	157	Engine failure	$650.00
479	12/7/1969	College Station, TX	21	24	69 Ford	192	0	Clutch	$1,025.00
480	1/18/1970	Riverside, CA	5	6	Plymouth SuperBird	186	2	Engine failure	$3,000.00
481	2/19/1970	Daytona Beach, FL	6	7	Plymouth SuperBird	50	0	Running	$400.00
482	2/22/1970	Daytona Beach, FL	39	11	Plymouth SuperBird	7	0	Engine failure	$1,105.00
483	3/1/1970	Richmond, VA	2	1	Plymouth	500	303	Running	$2,970.00
484	3/8/1970	Rockingham, NC	1	8	Plymouth SuperBird	492	188	Running	$16,715.00
485	3/15/1970	Savannah, GA	1	1	Plymouth	200	183	Running	$1,000.00
486	3/29/1970	Hampton, GA	5	4	Plymouth SuperBird	321	9	Running	$3,375.00
487	4/5/1970	Bristol, TN	24	3	Plymouth	37	0	Crash	$450.00
488	4/12/1970	Talladega, AL	7	8	Plymouth SuperBird	181	0	Running	$2,500.00
489	4/18/1970	North Wilkesboro, NC	1	16	Plymouth	400	349	Running	$6,025.00
490	4/30/1970	Columbia, SC	1	7	Plymouth	200	104	Running	$1,500.00
491	5/9/1970	Darlington, SC	18	12	Plymouth	176	3	Crash	$1,050.00
492	6/7/1970	Brooklyn, MI	28	2	Plymouth SuperBird	109	80	Ignition	$755.00
493	6/14/1970	Riverside, CA	1	2	Plymouth SuperBird	153	149	Running	$18,840.00
494	6/26/1970	Kingsport, TN	1	1	Plymouth	297	263	Running	$1,500.00
495	6/27/1970	Greenville, SC	19	2	Plymouth	137	1	Crash	$215.00
496	7/4/1970	Daytona Beach, FL	18	11	Plymouth SuperBird	139	0	Engine failure	$965.00
497	7/7/1970	Malta, NY	1	2	Plymouth	250	136	Running	$1,500.00
498	7/9/1970	Thompson, CT	2	2	Plymouth	200	11	Running	$1,800.00
499	7/12/1970	Trenton, NJ	1	4	Plymouth SuperBird	200	134	Running	$6,730.00
500	7/19/1970	Bristol, TN	5	6	Plymouth	464	0	Engine failure	$1,050.00
501	7/24/1970	Maryville, TN	1	1	Plymouth	200	172	Running	$1,500.00
502	7/25/1970	Nashville, TN	16	3	Plymouth	154	134	Crash	$730.00
503	8/2/1970	Hampton, GA	1	6	Plymouth SuperBird	328	295	Running	$19,600.00
504	8/6/1970	Columbia, SC	2	1	Plymouth	200	95	Running	$900.00
505	8/11/1970	Ona, WV	1	3	Plymouth	300	240	Running	$1,700.00
506	8/16/1970	Brooklyn, MI	14	3	Plymouth SuperBird	183	1	Running	$975.00
507	8/23/1970	Talladega, AL	7	5	Plymouth SuperBird	183	0	Running	$2,540.00
508	8/28/1970	Winston-Salem, NC	1	1	Plymouth	250	187	Running	$1,000.00
509	8/29/1970	South Boston, VA	1	1	Plymouth	281	271	Running	$1,500.00
510	9/7/1970	Darlington, SC	5	10	Plymouth SuperBird	362	0	Running	$3,100.00
511	9/11/1970	Hickory, NC	2	2	Plymouth	276	14	Running	$1,500.00
512	9/13/1970	Richmond, VA	1	1	Plymouth	500	488	Running	$4,675.00
513	9/20/1970	Dover, DE	1	2	Plymouth SuperBird	300	186	Running	$6,195.00
514	9/30/1970	Raleigh, NC	1	6	Plymouth	200	112	Running	$1,000.00
515	10/4/1970	North Wilkesboro, NC	2	3	Plymouth	400	216	Running	$2,850.00
516	10/11/1970	Charlotte, NC	23	2	Plymouth SuperBird	239	64	Crash	$2,039.00
517	10/18/1970	Martinsville, VA	1	4	Plymouth	500	480	Running	$8,775.00
518	11/8/1970	Macon, GA	1	1	Plymouth	500	113	Running	$3,275.00
519	11/15/1970	Rockingham, NC	6	7	Plymouth SuperBird	481	24	Running	$1,920.00
520	1/10/1971	Riverside, CA	20	1	Plymouth	107	62	Engine failure	$1,515.00
521	2/11/1971	Daytona Beach, FL	3	3	Plymouth	50	5	Running	$550.00
522	2/14/1971	Daytona Beach, FL	1	5	Plymouth	200	69	Running	$45,450.00
523	2/28/1971	Ontario, CA	3	3	Plymouth	200	13	Running	$12,825.00
524	3/7/1971	Richmond, VA	1	30	Plymouth	500	348	Running	$4,425.00
525	3/14/1971	Rockingham, NC	1	2	Plymouth	492	198	Running	$17,315.00
526	3/21/1971	Hickory, NC	1	4	Plymouth	276	161	Running	$2,200.00
527	3/28/1971	Bristol, TN	2	2	Plymouth	500	233	Running	$3,570.00
528	4/4/1971	Hampton, GA	2	3	Plymouth	328	59	Running	$10,700.00
529	4/8/1971	Columbia, SC	1	4	Plymouth	200	79	Running	$1,700.00
530	4/10/1971	Greenville, SC	7	4	Plymouth	196	0	Running	$705.00
531	4/15/1971	Maryville, TN	1	2	Plymouth	200	134	Running	$1,000.00
532	4/18/1971	North Wilkesboro, NC	1	3	Plymouth	400	186	Running	$4,545.00
533	4/25/1971	Martinsville, VA	1	3	Plymouth	500	118	Running	$5,075.00
534	5/2/1971	Darlington, SC	20	4	Plymouth	185	10	Engine failure	$925.00
535	5/9/1971	South Boston, VA	2	3	Plymouth	280	23	Running	$900.00
536	5/16/1971	Talladega, AL	38	5	Plymouth	42	0	Crash	$1,300.00
537	5/21/1971	Asheville, NC	1	1	Plymouth	300	252	Running	$1,500.00
538	5/23/1971	Kingsport, TN	17	2	Plymouth	166	6	Rear end	$290.00
539	5/30/1971	Charlotte, NC	4	5	Plymouth	398	0	Running	$7,175.00
540	6/6/1971	Dover, DE	3	1	Plymouth	498	30	Running	$5,020.00
541	6/13/1971	Brooklyn, MI	6	7	Plymouth	194	0	Running	$1,495.00
542	6/20/1971	Riverside, CA	13	2	Plymouth	110	4	Engine failure	$1,020.00
543	6/23/1971	Houston, TX	7	2	Plymouth	279	38	Running	$475.00
544	6/26/1971	Greenville, SC	1	2	Plymouth	200	89	Running	$1,500.00

545	7/4/1971	Daytona Beach, FL	2	4	Plymouth	160	46	Running	$8,825.00
546	7/11/1971	Bristol, TN	3	1	Plymouth	494	43	Running	$2,575.00
547	7/14/1971	Malta, NY	1	1	Plymouth	250	181	Running	$1,500.00
548	7/15/1971	Islip, NY	1	1	Plymouth	230	230	Running	$1,500.00
549	7/18/1971	Trenton, NJ	1	2	Plymouth	200	128	Running	$6,760.00
550	7/24/1971	Nashville, TN	1	1	Plymouth	420	400	Running	$4,325.00
551	8/1/1971	Hampton, GA	1	3	Plymouth	328	181	Running	$20,220.00
552	8/6/1971	Winston-Salem, NC	2	1	Plymouth	250	112	Running	$600.00
553	8/8/1971	Ona, WV	1	2	Plymouth	500	279	Running	$2,300.00
554	8/15/1971	Brooklyn, MI	2	6	Plymouth	197	30	Running	$7,870.00
555	8/22/1971	Talladega, AL	2	5	Plymouth	188	15	Running	$10,040.00
556	8/27/1971	Columbia, SC	1	1	Plymouth	200	110	Running	$1,500.00
557	8/28/1971	Hickory, NC	3	4	Plymouth	276	0	Running	$500.00
558	9/6/1971	Darlington, SC	2	6	Plymouth	366	13	Running	$10,050.00
559	9/26/1971	Martinsville, VA	3	2	Plymouth	499	1	Running	$2,200.00
560	10/10/1971	Charlotte, NC	4	5	Plymouth	238	9	Running	$4,025.00
561	10/17/1971	Dover, DE	1	4	Plymouth	500	101	Running	$14,570.00
562	10/24/1971	Rockingham, NC	1	5	Plymouth	492	189	Running	$17,120.00
563	11/14/1971	Richmond, VA	1	11	Plymouth	500	330	Running	$4,450.00
564	11/21/1971	North Wilkesboro, NC	3	2	Plymouth	400	306	Running	$1,650.00
565	12/12/1971	College Station, TX	1	3	Plymouth	250	111	Running	$13,395.00
566	1/23/1972	Riverside, CA	1	2	Plymouth	149	39	Running	$18,170.00
567	2/20/1972	Daytona Beach, FL	26	32	Plymouth	80	31	Valve	$5,060.00
568	2/27/1972	Richmond, VA	1	3	Plymouth	500	219	Running	$5,300.00
569	3/5/1972	Ontario, CA	4	3	Plymouth	199	17	Running	$9,970.00
570	3/12/1972	Rockingham, NC	2	2	Plymouth	491	12	Running	$11,825.00
571	3/26/1972	Atlanta, GA	6	3	Plymouth	325	31	Running	$5,480.00
572	4/9/1972	Bristol, TN	3	2	Plymouth	491	15	Running	$4,225.00
573	4/16/1972	Darlington, SC	2	3	Plymouth	292	27	Running	$10,375.00
574	4/23/1972	North Wilkesboro, NC	1	3	Plymouth	400	84	Running	$6,600.00
575	4/30/1972	Martinsville, VA	1	3	Plymouth	500	102	Running	$8,250.00
576	5/7/1972	Talladega, AL	5	3	Dodge	187	14	Running	$6,970.00
577	5/28/1972	Charlotte, NC	19	9	Dodge	328	0	Engine failure	$4,230.00
578	6/4/1972	Dover, DE	2	4	Dodge	499	240	Running	$10,375.00
579	6/11/1972	Brooklyn, MI	3	2	Dodge	200	18	Running	$6,925.00
580	6/18/1972	Riverside, CA	23	1	Plymouth	96	85	Engine failure	$3,295.00
581	6/25/1972	College Station, TX	1	1	Plymouth	250	186	Running	$16,245.00
582	7/4/1972	Daytona Beach, FL	2	4	Dodge	160	29	Running	$11,725.00
583	7/9/1972	Bristol, TN	2	2	Plymouth	497	51	Running	$5,700.00
584	7/16/1972	Trenton, NJ	3	3	Plymouth	199	27	Running	$3,800.00
585	7/23/1972	Atlanta, GA	2	5	Dodge	328	10	Running	$11,005.00
586	8/6/1972	Talladega, AL	7	3	Dodge	177	4	Running	$5,115.00
587	8/20/1972	Brooklyn, MI	4	1	Dodge	199	6	Running	$5,475.00
588	8/27/1972	Nashville, TN	2	2	Plymouth	420	136	Running	$5,010.00
589	9/4/1972	Darlington, SC	3	3	Dodge	360	4	Running	$8,990.00
590	9/10/1972	Richmond, VA	1	3	Plymouth	500	330	Running	$6,775.00
591	9/17/1972	Dover, DE	2	4	Plymouth	497	1	Running	$10,600.00
592	9/24/1972	Martinsville, VA	1	4	Plymouth	500	64	Running	$7,350.00
593	10/1/1972	North Wilkesboro, NC	1	3	Plymouth	400	160	Running	$7,200.00
594	10/8/1972	Charlotte, NC	10	8	Dodge	318	1	Crash	$3,965.00
595	10/22/1972	Rockingham, NC	2	3	Plymouth	490	53	Running	$12,050.00
596	11/12/1972	College Station, TX	3	3	Plymouth	250	97	Running	$8,220.00
597	1/21/1973	Riverside, CA	21	5	Dodge	95	39	Engine failure	$3,710.00
598	2/18/1973	Daytona Beach, FL	1	7	Dodge	200	17	Running	$36,100.00
599	2/25/1973	Richmond, VA	1	8	Dodge	500	227	Running	$6,350.00
600	3/18/1973	Rockingham, NC	23	3	Dodge	386	0	Engine failure	$3,345.00
601	3/25/1973	Bristol, TN	2	5	Dodge	498	0	Running	$5,305.00
602	4/1/1973	Atlanta, GA	34	16	Dodge	140	13	Engine failure	$3,430.00
603	4/8/1973	North Wilkesboro, NC	1	2	Dodge	400	387	Running	$6,230.00
604	4/15/1973	Darlington, SC	7	8	Dodge	340	4	Crash	$4,380.00
605	4/29/1973	Martinsville, VA	21	5	Dodge	334	0	Engine failure	$2,250.00
606	5/6/1973	Talladega, AL	35	3	Dodge	51	0	Crash	$3,880.00
607	5/12/1973	Nashville, TN	13	7	Dodge	385	0	Engine failure	$2,315.00
608	5/27/1973	Charlotte, NC	13	3	Dodge	370	134	Running	$6,600.00
609	6/3/1973	Dover, DE	4	13	Dodge	492	0	Running	$5,475.00
610	6/10/1973	College Station, TX	1	2	Dodge	250	77	Running	$17,820.00
611	6/17/1973	Riverside, CA	2	1	Dodge	153	57	Running	$10,275.00
612	6/24/1973	Brooklyn, MI	3	3	Dodge	199	5	Running	$6,800.00
613	7/4/1973	Daytona Beach, FL	2	4	Dodge	160	29	Running	$11,875.00
614	7/8/1973	Bristol, TN	21	4	Dodge	334	0	Ignition	$2,240.00
615	7/22/1973	Atlanta, GA	33	1	Dodge	72	0	Engine failure	$3,540.00
616	8/12/1973	Talladega, AL	14	3	Dodge	181	0	Running	$4,165.00
617	8/25/1973	Nashville, TN	2	8	Dodge	416	0	Running	$4,960.00
618	9/3/1973	Darlington, SC	4	3	Dodge	361	0	Running	$7,510.00
619	9/9/1973	Richmond, VA	1	5	Dodge	500	429	Running	$6,775.00
620	9/16/1973	Dover, DE	7	4	Dodge	480	15	Running	$4,250.00
621	9/23/1973	North Wilkesboro, NC	2	2	Dodge	400	222	Running	$4,800.00
622	9/30/1973	Martinsville, VA	1	6	Dodge	480	108	Running	$11,750.00
623	10/7/1973	Charlotte, NC	2	4	Dodge	334	52	Running	$17,275.00
624	10/21/1973	Rockingham, NC	35	1	Dodge	133	0	Camshaft	$3,550.00
625	1/26/1974	Riverside, CA	2	6	Dodge	191	0	Running	$12,825.00
626	2/17/1974	Daytona Beach, FL	1	2	Dodge	200	74	Running	$39,650.00
627	2/24/1974	Richmond, VA	2	3	Dodge	500	163	Running	$5,455.00
628	3/3/1974	Rockingham, NC	1	2	Dodge	492	278	Running	$18,025.00
629	3/17/1974	Bristol, TN	23	9	Dodge	109	0	Crash	$2,440.00
630	3/24/1974	Atlanta, GA	6	10	Dodge	325	17	Running	$5,500.00
631	4/7/1974	Darlington, SC	20	10	Dodge	255	0	Engine failure	$3,895.00
632	4/21/1974	North Wilkesboro, NC	1	4	Dodge	400	336	Running	$8,250.00
633	4/28/1974	Martinsville, VA	2	5	Dodge	500	0	Running	$8,000.00
634	5/5/1974	Talladega, AL	3	24	Dodge	188	0	Running	$11,245.00
635	5/12/1974	Nashville, TN	1	2	Dodge	420	107	Running	$7,900.00
636	5/19/1974	Dover, DE	3	2	Dodge	498	210	Engine failure	$8,250.00
637	5/26/1974	Charlotte, NC	2	2	Dodge	400	75	Running	$21,200.00

638	6/9/1974	Riverside, CA	25	4	Dodge	49	1	Engine failure	$3,740.00
639	6/16/1974	Brooklyn, MI	1	4	Dodge	180	80	Running	$17,190.00
640	7/4/1974	Daytona Beach, FL	2	6	Dodge	160	20	Running	$12,825.00
641	7/14/1974	Bristol, TN	3	1	Dodge	498	114	Running	$4,900.00
642	7/20/1974	Nashville, TN	13	3	Dodge	353	182	Crash	$2,715.00
643	7/28/1974	Atlanta, GA	1	2	Dodge	328	94	Running	$19,350.00
644	8/4/1974	Pocono, PA	1	3	Dodge	192	152	Running	$17,000.00
645	8/11/1974	Talladega, AL	1	3	Dodge	188	34	Running	$24,465.00
646	8/25/1974	Brooklyn, MI	2	4	Dodge	200	2	Running	$11,155.00
647	9/2/1974	Darlington, SC	35	1	Dodge	37	1	Crash	$4,350.00
648	9/8/1974	Richmond, VA	1	1	Dodge	500	383	Running	$8,740.00
649	9/15/1974	Dover, DE	1	2	Dodge	500	491	Running	$18,175.00
650	9/22/1974	North Wilkesboro, NC	2	1	Dodge	400	116	Running	$6,300.00
651	9/29/1974	Martinsville, VA	29	1	Dodge	22	0	Engine failure	$3,510.00
652	10/6/1974	Charlotte, NC	2	2	Dodge	334	2	Running	$13,475.00
653	10/20/1974	Rockingham, NC	3	1	Dodge	490	79	Running	$9,725.00
654	11/24/1974	Ontario, CA	15	1	Dodge	188	89	Engine failure	$5,475.00
655	1/19/1975	Riverside, CA	7	3	Dodge	172	4	Running	$6,185.00
656	2/16/1975	Daytona Beach, FL	7	4	Dodge	192	51	Running	$13,700.00
657	2/23/1975	Richmond, VA	1	1	Dodge	500	444	Running	$8,265.00
658	3/2/1975	Rockingham, NC	3	2	Dodge	483	78	Running	$10,925.00
659	3/16/1975	Bristol, TN	1	2	Dodge	500	243	Running	$7,350.00
660	3/23/1975	Atlanta, GA	1	1	Dodge	328	170	Running	$19,500.00
661	4/6/1975	North Wilkesboro, NC	1	2	Dodge	400	311	Running	$8,675.00
662	4/13/1975	Darlington, SC	26	3	Dodge	159	43	Crash	$4,345.00
663	4/27/1975	Martinsville, VA	1	6	Dodge	500	240	Running	$20,000.00
664	5/4/1975	Talladega, AL	19	5	Dodge	140	22	Wheel bearing	$6,375.00
665	5/10/1975	Nashville, TN	7	4	Dodge	404	0	Running	$3,350.00
666	5/18/1975	Dover, DE	3	3	Dodge	490	0	Running	$10,050.00
667	5/25/1975	Charlotte, NC	1	3	Dodge	400	234	Running	$30,290.00
668	6/8/1975	Riverside, CA	1	2	Dodge	153	60	Running	$18,135.00
669	6/15/1975	Brooklyn, MI	2	4	Dodge	200	65	Running	$13,130.00
670	7/4/1975	Daytona Beach, FL	1	13	Dodge	160	16	Running	$19,935.00
671	7/20/1975	Nashville, TN	2	4	Dodge	419	0	Running	$6,205.00
672	8/3/1975	Pocono, PA	2	6	Dodge	200	33	Running	$13,000.00
673	8/17/1975	Talladega, AL	2	7	Dodge	188	21	Running	$17,295.00
674	8/24/1975	Brooklyn, MI	1	4	Dodge	200	45	Running	$18,140.00
675	9/1/1975	Darlington, SC	2	4	Dodge	367	146	Running	$16,395.00
676	9/14/1975	Dover, DE	1	3	Dodge	500	250	Running	$18,250.00
677	9/21/1975	North Wilkesboro, NC	1	1	Dodge	400	184	Running	$9,960.00
678	9/28/1975	Martinsville, VA	22	6	Dodge	243	1	Rear end	$2,860.00
679	10/5/1975	Charlotte, NC	1	9	Dodge	334	168	Running	$30,970.00
680	10/12/1975	Richmond, VA	28	6	Dodge	34	0	Engine failure	$2,700.00
681	10/19/1975	Rockingham, NC	35	2	Dodge	20	4	Engine failure	$4,335.00
682	11/2/1975	Bristol, TN	1	4	Dodge	500	218	Running	$7,560.00
683	11/9/1975	Atlanta, GA	3	4	Dodge	328	118	Running	$10,725.00
684	11/23/1975	Ontario, CA	16	6	Dodge	168	29	Engine failure	$7,975.00
685	1/18/1976	Riverside, CA	25	27	Dodge	83	14	Engine failure	$5,660.00
686	2/15/1976	Daytona Beach, FL	2	6	Dodge	199	40	Running	$35,750.00
687	2/29/1976	Rockingham, NC	1	3	Dodge	492	362	Running	$19,915.00
688	3/7/1976	Richmond, VA	2	3	Dodge	400	122	Running	$8,025.00
689	3/14/1976	Bristol, TN	27	2	Dodge	64	0	Crash	$4,180.00
690	3/21/1976	Atlanta, GA	28	3	Dodge	194	7	Engine failure	$5,775.00
691	4/4/1976	North Wilkesboro, NC	2	7	Dodge	399	13	Running	$8,125.00
692	4/11/1976	Darlington, SC	23	9	Dodge	203	52	Engine failure	$5,625.00
693	4/25/1976	Martinsville, VA	4	9	Dodge	498	18	Running	$7,070.00
694	5/2/1976	Talladega, AL	4	2	Dodge	186	9	Running	$13,805.00
695	5/8/1976	Nashville, TN	2	7	Dodge	420	1	Running	$6,965.00
696	5/16/1976	Dover, DE	6	6	Dodge	492	0	Running	$7,055.00
697	5/30/1976	Charlotte, NC	2	2	Dodge	400	56	Running	$22,465.00
698	6/13/1976	Riverside, CA	9	7	Dodge	92	0	Running	$5,500.00
699	6/20/1976	Brooklyn, MI	4	1	Dodge	200	3	Running	$9,065.00
700	7/4/1976	Daytona Beach, FL	22	3	Dodge	126	1	Engine failure	$5,960.00
701	7/17/1976	Nashville, TN	2	2	Dodge	420	79	Running	$7,140.00
702	8/1/1976	Pocono, PA	1	5	Dodge	200	35	Running	$20,640.00
703	8/8/1976	Talladega, AL	20	14	Dodge	168	12	Engine failure	$7,230.00
704	8/22/1976	Brooklyn, MI	3	5	Dodge	200	22	Running	$10,985.00
705	8/29/1976	Bristol, TN	2	9	Dodge	398	0	Running	$7,800.00
706	9/6/1976	Darlington, SC	2	8	Dodge	367	32	Running	$18,055.00
707	9/12/1976	Richmond, VA	3	7	Dodge	399	3	Running	$7,180.00
708	9/19/1976	Dover, DE	2	2	Dodge	500	179	Running	$14,990.00
709	9/26/1976	Martinsville, VA	4	8	Dodge	338	0	Running	$7,070.00
710	10/3/1976	North Wilkesboro, NC	3	7	Dodge	399	0	Running	$6,705.00
711	10/10/1976	Charlotte, NC	8	3	Dodge	328	5	Running	$9,049.00
712	10/24/1976	Rockingham, NC	1	4	Dodge	492	193	Running	$20,395.00
713	11/7/1976	Atlanta, GA	28	4	Dodge	157	0	Engine failure	$5,430.00
714	11/21/1976	Ontario, CA	27	7	Dodge	127	11	Engine failure	$6,165.00
715	1/16/1977	Riverside, CA	3	9	Dodge	118	0	Running	$11,095.00
716	2/20/1977	Daytona Beach, FL	26	3	Dodge	111	4	Engine failure	$9,550.00
717	2/27/1977	Richmond, VA	6	2	Dodge	243	0	Running	$3,750.00
718	3/13/1977	Rockingham, NC	1	2	Dodge	492	281	Running	$18,594.00
719	3/20/1977	Atlanta, GA	1	1	Dodge	328	112	Running	$22,550.00
720	3/27/1977	North Wilkesboro, NC	2	7	Dodge	400	25	Running	$8,025.00
721	4/3/1977	Darlington, SC	3	7	Dodge	367	105	Running	$11,600.00
722	4/17/1977	Bristol, TN	3	3	Dodge	491	0	Running	$6,100.00
723	4/24/1977	Martinsville, VA	3	10	Dodge	381	1	Running	$7,750.00
724	5/1/1977	Talladega, AL	20	7	Dodge	153	19	Engine failure	$6,350.00
725	5/7/1977	Nashville, TN	5	4	Dodge	416	0	Running	$3,465.00
726	5/15/1977	Dover, DE	3	1	Dodge	499	51	Running	$9,830.00
727	5/29/1977	Charlotte, NC	1	2	Dodge	400	311	Running	$69,550.00
728	6/12/1977	Riverside, CA	1	1	Dodge	95	71	Running	$18,255.00
729	6/19/1977	Brooklyn, MI	2	3	Dodge	200	5	Running	$14,425.00
730	7/4/1977	Daytona Beach, FL	1	5	Dodge	160	95	Running	$23,075.00

731	7/17/1977	Nashville, TN	3	7	Dodge	418	10	Running	$4,965.00
732	7/31/1977	Pocono, PA	2	5	Dodge	200	9	Running	$12,200.00
733	8/7/1977	Talladega, AL	11	11	Dodge	180	1	Running	$6,120.00
734	8/22/1977	Brooklyn, MI	8	6	Dodge	198	2	Running	$5,100.00
735	8/28/1977	Bristol, TN	22	2	Dodge	118	1	Crash	$2,855.00
736	9/5/1977	Darlington, SC	4	6	Dodge	365	1	Running	$10,360.00
737	9/11/1977	Richmond, VA	2	3	Dodge	400	1	Running	$7,775.00
738	9/18/1977	Dover, DE	23	8	Dodge	301	0	Engine failure	$3,925.00
739	9/25/1977	Martinsville, VA	4	4	Dodge	499	0	Running	$5,850.00
740	10/2/1977	North Wilkesboro, NC	24	1	Dodge	240	199	Crash	$4,560.00
741	10/9/1977	Charlotte, NC	32	5	Dodge	107	25	Suspension	$4,415.00
742	10/23/1977	Rockingham, NC	2	5	Dodge	492	5	Running	$14,350.00
743	11/6/1977	Atlanta, GA	6	2	Dodge	268	10	Running	$7,600.00
744	11/20/1977	Ontario, CA	2	1	Dodge	200	59	Running	$17,535.00
745	1/22/1978	Riverside, CA	16	5	Dodge	104	0	Rear end	$5,100.00
746	2/19/1978	Daytona Beach, FL	33	6	Dodge	60	39	Crash	$11,600.00
747	2/26/1978	Richmond, VA	22	8	Dodge	356	0	Rear end	$3,175.00
748	3/5/1978	Rockingham, NC	4	10	Dodge	490	2	Running	$8,470.00
749	3/19/1978	Atlanta, GA	26	9	Dodge	278	0	Overheating	$4,655.00
750	4/2/1978	Bristol, TN	25	11	Dodge	47	0	Crash	$3,150.00
751	4/9/1978	Darlington, SC	5	10	Dodge	364	0	Running	$8,500.00
752	4/16/1978	North Wilkesboro, NC	2	7	Dodge	400	129	Running	$7,950.00
753	4/23/1978	Martinsville, VA	3	7	Dodge	497	0	Running	$8,700.00
754	5/14/1978	Talladega, AL	11	10	Dodge	183	2	Running	$7,700.00
755	5/21/1978	Dover, DE	7	15	Dodge	494	0	Running	$5,700.00
756	5/28/1978	Charlotte, NC	8	16	Dodge	398	0	Running	$10,140.00
757	6/3/1978	Nashville, TN	3	7	Dodge	416	0	Running	$5,265.00
758	6/11/1978	Riverside, CA	2	7	Dodge	95	4	Running	$14,200.00
759	6/18/1978	Brooklyn, MI	6	12	Dodge	199	0	Running	$6,690.00
760	7/4/1978	Daytona Beach, FL	4	7	Dodge	159	4	Running	$10,800.00
761	7/15/1978	Nashville, TN	23	12	Dodge	341	0	Engine failure	$3,025.00
762	7/30/1978	Pocono, PA	30	8	Dodge	152	7	Engine failure	$4,655.00
763	8/6/1978	Talladega, AL	7	6	Dodge	186	5	Running	$7,740.00
764	8/20/1978	Brooklyn, MI	14	14	Chevrolet	190	0	Crash	$5,075.00
765	8/26/1978	Bristol, TN	5	11	Chevrolet	495	2	Running	$4,350.00
766	9/4/1978	Darlington, SC	3	9	Chevrolet	366	1	Running	$13,175.00
767	9/10/1978	Richmond, VA	20	5	Chevrolet	356	13	Rear end	$3,250.00
768	9/17/1978	Dover, DE	27	11	Chevrolet	269	0	Ignition	$4,525.00
769	9/24/1978	Martinsville, VA	6	2	Chevrolet	496	0	Running	$5,200.00
770	10/1/1978	North Wilkesboro, NC	4	8	Chevrolet	397	0	Running	$4,875.00
771	10/8/1978	Charlotte, NC	27	9	Chevrolet	220	102	Ignition	$11,440.00
772	10/22/1978	Rockingham, NC	6	11	Chevrolet	485	18	Running	$7,000.00
773	11/5/1978	Atlanta, GA	2	11	Chevrolet	328	61	Running	$14,750.00
774	11/19/1978	Ontario, CA	34	3	Chevrolet	83	30	Engine failure	$4,555.00
775	1/14/1979	Riverside, CA	32	6	Chevrolet	14	0	Engine failure	$4,600.00
776	2/18/1979	Daytona Beach, FL	1	13	Oldsmobile	200	12	Running	$73,900.00
777	3/4/1979	Rockingham, NC	32	7	Chevrolet	9	0	Crash	$4,460.00
778	3/11/1979	Richmond, VA	5	7	Chevrolet	399	0	Running	$4,800.00
779	3/18/1979	Atlanta, GA	11	11	Oldsmobile	324	0	Running	$6,025.00
780	3/25/1979	North Wilkesboro, NC	2	7	Chevrolet	400	211	Running	$8,300.00
781	4/1/1979	Bristol, TN	4	13	Oldsmobile	498	0	Running	$5,850.00
782	4/8/1979	Darlington, SC	2	6	Chevrolet	367	89	Running	$16,100.00
783	4/22/1979	Martinsville, VA	1	2	Chevrolet	500	247	Running	$23,400.00
784	5/6/1979	Talladega, AL	4	7	Oldsmobile	185	0	Running	$13,100.00
785	5/12/1979	Nashville, TN	2	5	Chevrolet	420	164	Running	$8,150.00
786	5/20/1979	Dover, DE	30	15	Chevrolet	2	0	Crash	$4,250.00
787	5/27/1979	Charlotte, NC	2	2	Chevrolet	400	129	Running	$35,650.00
788	6/3/1979	College Station, TX	6	9	Chevrolet	195	0	Running	$8,700.00
789	6/10/1979	Riverside, CA	3	5	Chevrolet	95	0	Running	$10,350.00
790	6/17/1979	Brooklyn, MI	5	10	Chevrolet	200	23	Running	$8,325.00
791	7/4/1979	Daytona Beach, FL	5	11	Oldsmobile	158	2	Running	$9,480.00
792	7/14/1979	Nashville, TN	5	6	Chevrolet	406	0	Running	$4,280.00
793	7/30/1979	Pocono, PA	2	10	Chevrolet	200	17	Running	$15,465.00
794	8/5/1979	Talladega, AL	4	13	Oldsmobile	186	4	Running	$11,475.00
795	8/19/1979	Brooklyn, MI	1	5	Chevrolet	200	9	Running	$21,100.00
796	8/25/1979	Bristol, TN	2	1	Chevrolet	500	77	Running	$10,100.00
797	9/3/1979	Darlington, SC	9	4	Chevrolet	361	0	Running	$7,800.00
798	9/9/1979	Richmond, VA	6	7	Chevrolet	398	0	Running	$6,300.00
799	9/16/1979	Dover, DE	1	4	Chevrolet	500	110	Running	$21,650.00
800	9/23/1979	Martinsville, VA	2	6	Chevrolet	500	0	Running	$12,550.00
801	10/7/1979	Charlotte, NC	4	9	Chevrolet	332	11	Running	$15,375.00
802	10/14/1979	North Wilkesboro, NC	3	11	Chevrolet	399	0	Running	$6,500.00
803	10/21/1979	Rockingham, NC	1	7	Chevrolet	492	139	Running	$20,960.00
804	11/4/1979	Atlanta, GA	6	13	Chevrolet	327	0	Running	$8,450.00
805	11/18/1979	Ontario, CA	5	5	Chevrolet	200	6	Running	$9,025.00
806	1/19/1980	Riverside, CA	3	3	Chevrolet	119	13	Running	$15,100.00
807	2/17/1980	Daytona Beach, FL	25	4	Oldsmobile	157	4	Clutch	$15,100.00
808	2/24/1980	Richmond, VA	3	3	Chevrolet	400	70	Running	$9,375.00
809	3/9/1980	Rockingham, NC	2	9	Chevrolet	492	39	Running	$18,720.00
810	3/16/1980	Atlanta, GA	33	8	Chevrolet	117	3	Engine failure	$7,100.00
811	3/30/1980	Bristol, TN	8	7	Chevrolet	492	1	Running	$6,400.00
812	4/13/1980	Darlington, SC	9	7	Chevrolet	184	0	Running	$9,550.00
813	4/20/1980	North Wilkesboro, NC	1	7	Chevrolet	400	327	Running	$18,925.00
814	4/27/1980	Martinsville, VA	3	8	Chevrolet	500	72	Running	$13,475.00
815	5/4/1980	Talladega, AL	31	10	Oldsmobile	57	0	Engine failure	$8,730.00
816	5/10/1980	Nashville, TN	1	6	Chevrolet	420	96	Running	$15,350.00
817	5/18/1980	Dover, DE	2	9	Chevrolet	500	10	Running	$16,775.00
818	5/25/1980	Charlotte, NC	4	9	Chevrolet	397	3	Running	$19,550.00
819	6/1/1980	College Station, TX	2	6	Chevrolet	199	0	Running	$16,800.00
820	6/8/1980	Riverside, CA	8	6	Chevrolet	93	0	Running	$8,000.00
821	6/15/1980	Brooklyn, MI	5	8	Chevrolet	199	0	Running	$13,075.00
822	7/4/1980	Daytona Beach, FL	5	22	Oldsmobile	160	0	Running	$12,130.00
823	7/12/1980	Nashville, TN	5	10	Chevrolet	416	17	Running	$6,630.00

824	7/27/1980	Pocono, PA	33	3	Chevrolet	56	18	Crash	$7,450.00
825	8/3/1980	Talladega, AL	18	5	Oldsmobile	154	5	Engine failure	$8,915.00
826	8/17/1980	Brooklyn, MI	5	12	Chevrolet	200	4	Running	$11,075.00
827	8/23/1980	Bristol, TN	4	3	Chevrolet	499	10	Running	$7,700.00
828	9/1/1980	Darlington, SC	9	15	Chevrolet	365	2	Running	$10,475.00
829	9/7/1980	Richmond, VA	2	9	Chevrolet	400	2	Running	$13,350.00
830	9/14/1980	Dover, DE	17	12	Chevrolet	468	4	Engine failure	$7,465.00
831	9/21/1980	North Wilkesboro, NC	18	14	Chevrolet	361	0	Running	$5,725.00
832	9/28/1980	Martinsville, VA	15	12	Chevrolet	443	1	Running	$5,800.00
833	10/5/1980	Charlotte, NC	27	19	Chevrolet	252	1	Engine failure	$7,375.00
834	10/19/1980	Rockingham, NC	14	13	Chevrolet	461	10	Running	$7,800.00
835	11/2/1980	Atlanta, GA	21	15	Chevrolet	256	1	Engine failure	$7,125.00
836	11/15/1980	Ontario, CA	30	8	Chevrolet	97	0	Engine failure	$7,325.00
837	1/11/1981	Riverside, CA	5	17	Chevrolet	119	4	Running	$4,250.00
838	2/15/1981	Daytona Beach, FL	1	8	Buick	200	26	Running	$90,575.00
839	2/22/1981	Richmond, VA	3	3	Buick	399	39	Running	$9,775.00
840	3/1/1981	Rockingham, NC	3	3	Buick	492	25	Running	$14,370.00
841	3/15/1981	Atlanta, GA	38	14	Buick	113	34	Engine failure	$6,370.00
842	3/29/1981	Bristol, TN	29	9	Buick	116	1	Engine failure	$5,010.00
843	4/5/1981	North Wilkesboro, NC	1	13	Buick	400	89	Running	$18,850.00
844	4/12/1981	Darlington, SC	33	9	Buick	25	0	Oil pan	$6,465.00
845	4/26/1981	Martinsville, VA	28	15	Buick	40	0	Crash	$5,070.00
846	5/3/1981	Talladega, AL	39	21	Buick	1	0	Crash	$6,735.00
847	5/9/1981	Nashville, TN	4	7	Buick	419	0	Running	$6,950.00
848	5/17/1981	Dover, DE	19	9	Buick	368	3	Rear end	$6,570.00
849	5/24/1981	Charlotte, NC	24	3	Buick	296	4	Engine failure	$11,700.00
850	6/7/1981	College Station, TX	4	5	Buick	199	0	Running	$12,550.00
851	6/14/1981	Riverside, CA	3	3	Buick	95	25	Running	$12,200.00
852	6/21/1981	Brooklyn, MI	6	12	Buick	200	1	Running	$8,950.00
853	7/4/1981	Daytona Beach, FL	3	14	Buick	160	7	Running	$17,200.00
854	7/11/1981	Nashville, TN	9	9	Buick	417	0	Running	$5,675.00
855	7/26/1981	Pocono, PA	2	4	Buick	200	36	Running	$18,915.00
856	8/2/1981	Talladega, AL	40	20	Buick	12	0	Oil pan	$6,650.00
857	8/16/1981	Brooklyn, MI	1	7	Buick	200	64	Running	$23,750.00
858	8/22/1981	Bristol, TN	24	10	Buick	73	0	Cylinder head	$5,060.00
859	9/7/1981	Darlington, SC	30	8	Buick	278	31	Engine failure	$8,000.00
860	9/13/1981	Richmond, VA	11	21	Buick	395	3	Running	$5,660.00
861	9/20/1981	Dover, DE	10	11	Buick	494	2	Running	$7,575.00
862	9/27/1981	Martinsville, VA	18	16	Buick	357	0	Engine failure	$5,200.00
863	10/4/1981	North Wilkesboro, NC	21	9	Buick	210	1	Crash	$5,425.00
864	10/11/1981	Charlotte, NC	30	9	Buick	180	15	Engine failure	$9,125.00
865	11/1/1981	Rockingham, NC	4	12	Buick	492	92	Running	$10,400.00
866	11/8/1981	Atlanta, GA	26	3	Buick	207	44	Engine failure	$6,380.00
867	11/22/1981	Riverside, CA	7	25	Buick	119	0	Running	$8,100.00
868	2/14/1982	Daytona Beach, FL	27	21	Pontiac	103	0	Crash	$14,300.00
869	2/21/1982	Richmond, VA	2	15	Pontiac	250	1	Running	$16,325.00
870	3/14/1982	Bristol, TN	7	16	Pontiac	497	7	Running	$9,430.00
871	3/21/1982	Atlanta, GA	2	5	Pontiac	287	13	Running	$37,725.00
872	3/28/1982	Rockingham, NC	30	15	Pontiac	119	1	Crash	$8,660.00
873	4/4/1982	Darlington, SC	31	17	Pontiac	89	1	Engine failure	$9,150.00
874	4/18/1982	North Wilkesboro, NC	5	19	Pontiac	399	2	Running	$10,000.00
875	4/25/1982	Martinsville, VA	15	19	Pontiac	394	2	Rear end	$7,525.00
876	5/2/1982	Talladega, AL	27	9	Pontiac	82	0	Fuel pump	$10,065.00
877	5/8/1982	Nashville, TN	9	16	Pontiac	416	0	Running	$7,835.00
878	5/16/1982	Dover, DE	24	14	Pontiac	181	0	Engine failure	$8,650.00
879	5/30/1982	Charlotte, NC	8	21	Pontiac	394	1	Running	$14,425.00
880	6/6/1982	Pocono, PA	7	10	Pontiac	199	73	Running	$11,925.00
881	6/13/1982	Riverside, CA	36	10	Pontiac	17	0	Engine failure	$8,375.00
882	6/20/1982	Brooklyn, MI	26	9	Pontiac	178	9	Engine failure	$9,360.00
883	7/4/1982	Daytona Beach, FL	25	10	Pontiac	135	5	Crash	$10,375.00
884	7/10/1982	Nashville, TN	7	15	Pontiac	418	0	Running	$8,235.00
885	7/25/1982	Pocono, PA	2	11	Pontiac	200	72	Running	$21,500.00
886	8/1/1982	Talladega, AL	3	13	Pontiac	188	27	Running	$26,975.00
887	8/22/1982	Brooklyn, MI	2	11	Pontiac	200	13	Running	$20,505.00
888	8/28/1982	Bristol, TN	26	14	Pontiac	50	0	Steering	$7,475.00
889	9/6/1982	Darlington, SC	2	8	Pontiac	367	20	Running	$26,165.00
890	9/12/1982	Richmond, VA	13	11	Pontiac	394	0	Running	$8,270.00
891	9/19/1982	Dover, DE	30	8	Pontiac	160	40	Steering	$8,500.00
892	10/3/1982	North Wilkesboro, NC	4	16	Pontiac	399	0	Running	$11,125.00
893	10/10/1982	Charlotte, NC	8	8	Pontiac	328	0	Running	$13,420.00
894	10/17/1982	Martinsville, VA	3	17	Pontiac	500	0	Running	$14,925.00
895	10/31/1982	Rockingham, NC	6	19	Pontiac	491	14	Running	$11,100.00
896	11/7/1982	Atlanta, GA	15	13	Pontiac	312	54	Engine failure	$10,000.00
897	11/21/1982	Riverside, CA	31	11	Pontiac	87	0	Clutch	$8,550.00
898	2/20/1983	Daytona Beach, FL	38	6	Pontiac	47	29	Engine failure	$22,600.00
899	2/27/1983	Richmond, VA	8	10	Pontiac	398	0	Running	$7,210.00
900	3/13/1983	Rockingham, NC	1	12	Pontiac	492	48	Running	$24,150.00
901	3/27/1983	Atlanta, GA	5	11	Pontiac	328	76	Running	$12,650.00
902	4/10/1983	Darlington, SC	25	18	Pontiac	269	0	Crash	$7,675.00
903	4/17/1983	North Wilkesboro, NC	10	23	Pontiac	398	1	Running	$6,510.00
904	4/24/1983	Martinsville, VA	17	9	Pontiac	434	1	Crash	$5,875.00
905	5/1/1983	Talladega, AL	1	15	Pontiac	188	52	Running	$46,650.00
906	5/7/1983	Nashville, TN	6	18	Pontiac	415	0	Running	$6,800.00
907	5/15/1983	Dover, DE	7	14	Pontiac	493	1	Running	$9,000.00
908	5/21/1983	Bristol, TN	5	11	Pontiac	498	0	Running	$7,930.00
909	5/29/1983	Charlotte, NC	2	17	Pontiac	400	4	Running	$31,450.00
910	6/5/1983	Riverside, CA	10	8	Pontiac	93	0	Running	$8,250.00
911	6/12/1983	Pocono, PA	3	10	Pontiac	200	21	Running	$17,225.00
912	6/19/1983	Brooklyn, MI	11	19	Pontiac	200	0	Running	$10,050.00
913	7/4/1983	Daytona Beach, FL	33	30	Pontiac	78	0	Crash	$7,225.00
914	7/16/1983	Nashville, TN	19	16	Pontiac	392	0	Running	$5,575.00
915	7/24/1983	Pocono, PA	10	9	Pontiac	200	5	Running	$9,750.00
916	7/31/1983	Talladega, AL	4	12	Pontiac	188	3	Running	$17,475.00

917	8/21/1983	Brooklyn, MI	6	20	Pontiac	200	3	Running	$11,640.00
918	8/27/1983	Bristol, TN	9	14	Pontiac	407	0	Running	$6,400.00
919	9/5/1983	Darlington, SC	12	21	Pontiac	363	0	Running	$9,700.00
920	9/11/1983	Richmond, VA	6	17	Pontiac	396	0	Running	$8,080.00
921	9/18/1983	Dover, DE	9	17	Pontiac	491	1	Running	$8,385.00
922	9/25/1983	Martinsville, VA	9	10	Pontiac	489	0	Running	$6,500.00
923	10/2/1983	North Wilkesboro, NC	12	14	Pontiac	396	0	Running	$5,950.00
924	10/9/1983	Charlotte, NC	1	20	Pontiac	334	23	Running	$40,400.00
925	10/30/1983	Rockingham, NC	26	17	Pontiac	208	0	Crash	$7,205.00
926	11/6/1983	Atlanta, GA	5	11	Pontiac	326	1	Running	$12,100.00
927	11/20/1983	Riverside, CA	10	8	Pontiac	118	10	Running	$8,650.00
928	2/19/1984	Daytona Beach, FL	31	34	Pontiac	92	24	Cam shaft	$10,150.00
929	2/26/1984	Richmond, VA	15	15	Pontiac	396	0	Running	$1,995.00
930	3/4/1984	Rockingham, NC	4	18	Pontiac	491	0	Running	$5,545.00
931	3/18/1984	Atlanta, GA	4	10	Pontiac	327	0	Running	$8,650.00
932	4/1/1984	Bristol, TN	8	16	Pontiac	498	0	Running	$2,630.00
933	4/8/1984	North Wilkesboro, NC	12	13	Pontiac	397	0	Running	$1,330.00
934	4/15/1984	Darlington, SC	7	17	Pontiac	364	7	Running	$7,900.00
935	4/29/1984	Martinsville, VA	12	17	Pontiac	493	0	Running	$4,295.00
936	5/6/1984	Talladega, AL	6	13	Pontiac	187	18	Running	$18,495.00
937	5/12/1984	Nashville, TN	7	12	Pontiac	420	17	Running	$5,225.00
938	5/20/1984	Dover, DE	1	5	Pontiac	500	129	Running	$28,105.00
939	5/27/1984	Charlotte, NC	34	8	Pontiac	216	0	Engine failure	$4,390.00
940	6/3/1984	Riverside, CA	23	10	Pontiac	81	16	Running	$2,580.00
941	6/10/1984	Pocono, PA	13	7	Pontiac	199	11	Running	$6,925.00
942	6/17/1984	Brooklyn, MI	34	21	Pontiac	120	0	Fuel pump	$4,655.00
943	7/4/1984	Daytona Beach, FL	1	6	Pontiac	160	53	Running	$43,755.00
944	7/14/1984	Nashville, TN	25	3	Pontiac	212	0	Engine failure	$2,485.00
945	7/22/1984	Pocono, PA	27	14	Pontiac	136	0	Valve	$4,105.00
946	7/29/1984	Talladega, AL	23	11	Pontiac	157	0	Running	$5,625.00
947	8/12/1984	Brooklyn, MI	9	22	Pontiac	199	0	Running	$8,875.00
948	8/25/1984	Bristol, TN	17	19	Pontiac	440	0	Running	$3,180.00
949	9/2/1984	Darlington, SC	29	16	Pontiac	129	0	Engine failure	$4,935.00
950	9/9/1984	Richmond, VA	5	9	Pontiac	399	0	Running	$7,730.00
951	9/16/1984	Dover, DE	37	11	Pontiac	92	0	Oil pump	$2,250.00
952	9/23/1984	Martinsville, VA	8	21	Pontiac	494	0	Running	$5,450.00
953	10/7/1984	Charlotte, NC	9	23	Pontiac	332	0	Running	$8,900.00
954	10/14/1984	North Wilkesboro, NC	18	28	Pontiac	392	0	Running	$3,285.00
955	10/21/1984	Rockingham, NC	15	12	Pontiac	468	0	Running	$5,585.00
956	11/11/1984	Atlanta, GA	8	15	Pontiac	327	0	Running	$8,055.00
957	11/18/1984	Riverside, CA	14	17	Pontiac	117	0	Running	$5,435.00
958	2/17/1985	Daytona Beach, FL	34	8	Pontiac	80	2	Clutch	$18,040.00
959	2/24/1985	Richmond, VA	26	12	Pontiac	107	0	Crash	$6,340.00
960	3/3/1985	Rockingham, NC	8	13	Pontiac	491	0	Running	$10,810.00
961	3/17/1985	Atlanta, GA	13	24	Pontiac	319	0	Running	$9,625.00
962	4/6/1985	Bristol, TN	8	15	Pontiac	495	0	Running	$7,450.00
963	4/14/1985	Darlington, SC	33	18	Pontiac	121	0	Engine failure	$7,760.00
964	4/21/1985	North Wilkesboro, NC	21	11	Pontiac	389	0	Running	$6,235.00
965	4/28/1985	Martinsville, VA	7	20	Pontiac	498	0	Running	$8,400.00
966	5/5/1985	Talladega, AL	27	9	Pontiac	94	1	Valve	$9,370.00
967	5/19/1985	Dover, DE	7	7	Pontiac	494	0	Running	$11,600.00
968	5/26/1985	Charlotte, NC	26	29	Pontiac	310	0	Engine failure	$9,050.00
969	6/2/1985	Riverside, CA	7	20	Pontiac	95	1	Running	$9,200.00
970	6/9/1985	Pocono, PA	33	16	Pontiac	67	0	Valve	$8,060.00
971	6/16/1985	Brooklyn, MI	30	16	Pontiac	158	3	Engine failure	$8,170.00
972	7/4/1985	Daytona Beach, FL	29	8	Pontiac	64	0	Crash	$9,475.00
973	7/21/1985	Pocono, PA	27	15	Pontiac	178	0	Engine failure	$8,415.00
974	7/28/1985	Talladega, AL	6	29	Pontiac	187	0	Running	$15,600.00
975	8/11/1985	Brooklyn, MI	37	18	Pontiac	79	0	Engine failure	$6,725.00
976	8/24/1985	Bristol, TN	8	24	Pontiac	496	0	Running	$7,650.00
977	9/1/1985	Darlington, SC	12	24	Pontiac	364	0	Running	$10,860.00
978	9/8/1985	Richmond, VA	3	19	Pontiac	400	83	Running	$14,625.00
979	9/15/1985	Dover, DE	9	13	Pontiac	492	1	Running	$10,600.00
980	9/22/1985	Martinsville, VA	22	14	Pontiac	334	0	Transmission	$6,405.00
981	9/29/1985	North Wilkesboro, NC	8	22	Pontiac	398	0	Running	$7,295.00
982	10/6/1985	Charlotte, NC	10	23	Pontiac	330	0	Running	$12,450.00
983	10/25/1985	Rockingham, NC	33	23	Pontiac	282	14	Engine failure	$7,800.00
984	11/3/1985	Atlanta, GA	10	5	Pontiac	326	0	Running	$10,675.00
985	11/17/1985	Riverside, CA	8	21	Pontiac	119	0	Running	$9,900.00
986	2/16/1986	Daytona Beach, FL	36	10	Pontiac	63	0	Crash	$10,790.00
987	2/23/1986	Richmond, VA	20	27	Pontiac	363	0	Running	$1,615.00
988	3/2/1986	Rockingham, NC	3	13	Pontiac	492	59	Running	$15,970.00
989	3/16/1986	Atlanta, GA	11	11	Pontiac	327	2	Running	$8,220.00
990	4/6/1986	Bristol, TN	14	11	Pontiac	491	0	Running	$4,760.00
991	4/13/1986	Darlington, SC	7	16	Pontiac	364	0	Running	$9,600.00
992	4/20/1986	North Wilkesboro, NC	29	2	Pontiac	131	11	Engine failure	$7,495.00
993	4/27/1986	Martinsville, VA	28	8	Pontiac	202	0	Axle	$3,315.00
994	5/4/1986	Talladega, AL	7	18	Pontiac	188	0	Running	$14,425.00
995	5/18/1986	Dover, DE	6	4	Pontiac	494	0	Running	$10,480.00
996	5/25/1986	Charlotte, NC	38	37	Chevrolet	123	0	Engine failure	$5,465.00
997	6/1/1986	Riverside, CA	6	7	Pontiac	95	0	Running	$7,745.00
998	6/8/1986	Pocono, PA	19	13	Pontiac	195	0	Running	$5,770.00
999	6/15/1986	Brooklyn, MI	13	15	Pontiac	199	0	Running	$8,625.00
1000	7/4/1986	Daytona Beach, FL	22	19	Pontiac	156	0	Running	$6,595.00
1001	7/20/1986	Pocono, PA	34	7	Pontiac	120	0	Crash	$4,270.00
1002	7/27/1986	Talladega, AL	37	24	Pontiac	51	5	Crash	$5,080.00
1003	8/10/1986	Watkins Glen, NY	10	9	Pontiac	90	0	Running	$10,550.00
1004	8/17/1986	Brooklyn, MI	18	30	Pontiac	194	0	Engine failure	$6,705.00
1005	8/23/1986	Bristol, TN	7	14	Pontiac	497	0	Running	$6,380.00
1006	8/31/1986	Darlington, SC	40	19	Pontiac	6	0	Crash	$3,470.00
1007	9/7/1986	Richmond, VA	4	16	Pontiac	400	37	Running	$10,260.00
1008	9/14/1986	Dover, DE	12	16	Pontiac	493	0	Running	$6,555.00
1009	9/21/1986	Martinsville, VA	16	18	Pontiac	490	0	Running	$4,970.00

1010	9/28/1986	North Wilkesboro, NC	3	19	Pontiac	400	38	Running	$12,105.00
1011	10/5/1986	Charlotte, NC	35	31	Pontiac	89	0	Overheating	$4,135.00
1012	10/19/1986	Rockingham, NC	8	13	Pontiac	491	1	Running	$9,105.00
1013	11/2/1986	Atlanta, GA	2	15	Pontiac	327	0	Running	$26,130.00
1014	11/16/1986	Riverside, CA	21	7	Pontiac	108	0	Engine failure	$4,820.00
1015	2/15/1987	Daytona Beach, FL	3	11	Pontiac	200	2	Running	$76,040.00
1016	3/1/1987	Rockingham, NC	15	13	Pontiac	486	0	Running	$8,175.00
1017	3/8/1987	Richmond, VA	23	15	Pontiac	317	0	Running	$3,480.00
1018	3/15/1987	Atlanta, GA	14	17	Pontiac	325	1	Running	$7,215.00
1019	3/29/1987	Darlington, SC	3	24	Pontiac	367	1	Running	$20,450.00
1020	4/5/1987	North Wilkesboro, NC	6	15	Pontiac	399	1	Running	$6,435.00
1021	4/12/1987	Bristol, TN	2	18	Pontiac	500	1	Running	$21,030.00
1022	4/26/1987	Martinsville, VA	22	10	Pontiac	347	0	Timing belt	$4,375.00
1023	5/3/1987	Talladega, AL	16	25	Pontiac	173	0	Running	$9,030.00
1024	5/24/1987	Charlotte, NC	4	28	Pontiac	398	0	Running	$24,925.00
1025	5/31/1987	Dover, DE	36	24	Pontiac	69	0	Crash	$3,175.00
1026	6/14/1987	Pocono, PA	29	18	Pontiac	171	0	Crash	$5,580.00
1027	6/21/1987	Riverside, CA	6	15	Pontiac	95	0	Running	$7,795.00
1028	6/28/1987	Brooklyn, MI	12	14	Pontiac	199	0	Running	$9,425.00
1029	7/4/1987	Daytona Beach, FL	26	21	Pontiac	155	0	Running	$5,650.00
1030	7/19/1987	Pocono, PA	8	22	Pontiac	199	0	Running	$9,500.00
1031	7/26/1987	Talladega, AL	37	28	Pontiac	47	0	Engine failure	$5,040.00
1032	8/10/1987	Watkins Glen, NY	14	22	Pontiac	90	0	Running	$7,655.00
1033	8/16/1987	Brooklyn, MI	11	11	Pontiac	199	28	Crash	$9,990.00
1034	8/22/1987	Bristol, TN	5	20	Pontiac	500	2	Running	$10,030.00
1035	9/6/1987	Darlington, SC	3	14	Pontiac	202	2	Running	$22,530.00
1036	9/13/1987	Richmond, VA	5	17	Pontiac	399	0	Running	$10,180.00
1037	9/20/1987	Dover, DE	9	26	Pontiac	496	0	Running	$8,575.00
1038	9/27/1987	Martinsville, VA	13	16	Pontiac	484	0	Running	$4,720.00
1039	10/4/1987	North Wilkesboro, NC	9	19	Pontiac	397	0	Running	$5,310.00
1040	10/11/1987	Charlotte, NC	5	41	Pontiac	333	0	Running	$31,860.00
1041	10/25/1987	Rockingham, NC	17	36	Pontiac	486	0	Running	$6,300.00
1042	11/8/1987	Riverside, CA	4	16	Pontiac	119	0	Running	$13,780.00
1043	11/22/1987	Atlanta, GA	30	30	Pontiac	154	0	Crash	$5,600.00
1044	2/14/1988	Daytona Beach, FL	34	34	Pontiac	104	0	Crash	$11,475.00
1045	2/21/1988	Richmond, VA	3	9	Pontiac	400	0	Running	$16,975.00
1046	3/6/1988	Rockingham, NC	41	20	Pontiac	17	0	Crash	$4,140.00
1047	3/20/1988	Atlanta, GA	23	24	Pontiac	285	0	Engine failure	$5,615.00
1048	3/27/1988	Darlington, SC	41	30	Pontiac	4	0	Crash	$3,960.00
1049	4/10/1988	Bristol, TN	6	17	Pontiac	497	0	Running	$9,800.00
1050	4/17/1988	North Wilkesboro, NC	6	9	Pontiac	398	0	Running	$9,560.00
1051	4/24/1988	Martinsville, VA	32	27	Pontiac	31	0	Engine failure	$3,510.00
1052	5/1/1988	Talladega, AL	20	32	Pontiac	185	0	Running	$8,970.00
1053	5/29/1988	Charlotte, NC	15	30	Pontiac	392	1	Running	$10,985.00
1054	6/5/1988	Dover, DE	15	19	Pontiac	495	0	Running	$6,275.00
1055	6/12/1988	Riverside, CA	6	29	Pontiac	95	0	Running	$10,850.00
1056	6/19/1988	Pocono, PA	26	13	Pontiac	147	10	Crash	$5,256.00
1057	6/26/1988	Brooklyn, MI	24	24	Pontiac	186	0	Running	$6,265.00
1058	7/2/1988	Daytona Beach, FL	20	27	Pontiac	159	0	Running	$7,230.00
1059	7/24/1988	Pocono, PA	28	15	Pontiac	161	1	Engine failure	$6,525.00
1060	7/31/1988	Talladega, AL	21	34	Pontiac	187	0	Running	$6,635.00
1061	8/14/1988	Watkins Glen, NY	17	12	Pontiac	90	0	Running	$6,200.00
1062	8/21/1988	Brooklyn, MI	39	24	Pontiac	68	0	Distributor	$4,825.00
1063	8/27/1988	Bristol, TN	8	20	Pontiac	497	0	Running	$6,300.00
1064	9/4/1988	Darlington, SC	33	26	Pontiac	266	0	Engine failure	$4,925.00
1065	9/11/1988	Richmond, VA	34	32	Pontiac	26	0	Crash	$2,900.00
1066	9/18/1988	Dover, DE	38	22	Pontiac	72	0	Engine failure	$4,070.00
1067	9/25/1988	Martinsville, VA	27	27	Pontiac	313	0	Running	$3,525.00
1068	10/9/1988	Charlotte, NC	38	33	Pontiac	58	0	Crash	$4,145.00
1069	10/16/1988	North Wilkesboro, NC	18	16	Pontiac	397	0	Running	$4,420.00
1070	10/23/1988	Rockingham, NC	25	35	Pontiac	425	0	Engine failure	$5,090.00
1071	11/6/1988	Phoenix, AZ	35	30	Pontiac	168	0	Oil pan	$4,435.00
1072	11/20/1988	Atlanta, GA	36	20	Pontiac	84	0	Crash	$2,195.00
1073	2/19/1989	Daytona Beach, FL	17	34	Pontiac	198	0	Running	$19,335.00
1074	3/5/1989	Rockingham, NC	16	38	Pontiac	487	0	Running	$5,700.00
1075	3/19/1989	Atlanta, GA	27	24	Pontiac	257	9	Engine failure	$3,295.00
1076	4/2/1989	Darlington, SC	15	33	Pontiac	364	0	Running	$4,955.00
1077	4/23/1989	Martinsville, VA	24	17	Pontiac	420	0	Running	$2,570.00
1078	5/7/1989	Talladega, AL	23	15	Pontiac	186	0	Running	$5,360.00
1079	5/28/1989	Charlotte, NC	19	11	Pontiac	391	0	Running	$6,400.00
1080	6/4/1989	Dover, DE	20	30	Pontiac	489	0	Running	$4,375.00
1081	6/11/1989	Sonoma, CA	26	38	Pontiac	72	0	Running	$3,345.00
1082	6/18/1989	Pocono, PA	25	19	Pontiac	189	0	Running	$3,775.00
1083	6/25/1989	Brooklyn, MI	30	31	Pontiac	170	0	Engine failure	$4,755.00
1084	7/1/1989	Daytona Beach, FL	20	26	Pontiac	158	0	Running	$6,505.00
1085	7/23/1989	Pocono, PA	38	25	Pontiac	22	0	Engine failure	$2,875.00
1086	7/30/1989	Talladega, AL	21	26	Pontiac	186	0	Running	$5,770.00
1087	8/13/1989	Watkins Glen, NY	13	25	Pontiac	90	0	Running	$5,760.00
1088	8/20/1989	Brooklyn, MI	18	17	Pontiac	198	0	Running	$5,750.00
1089	9/3/1989	Darlington, SC	35	33	Pontiac	91	0	Engine failure	$2,995.00
1090	9/10/1989	Richmond, VA	33	35	Pontiac	76	0	Clutch	$2,925.00
1091	9/17/1989	Dover, DE	30	32	Pontiac	351	0	Fatigue	$2,850.00
1092	9/24/1989	Martinsville, VA	24	30	Pontiac	357	0	Crash	$3,220.00
1093	10/8/1989	Charlotte, NC	34	27	Pontiac	142	0	Engine failure	$2,410.00
1094	10/15/1989	North Wilkesboro, NC	32	29	Pontiac	124	0	Crash	$2,330.00
1095	10/22/1989	Rockingham, NC	34	34	Pontiac	247	0	Handling	$4,280.00
1096	11/5/1989	Phoenix, AZ	42	26	Pontiac	34	0	Engine failure	$2,840.00
1097	11/19/1989	Atlanta, GA	28	35	Pontiac	268	0	A-frame	$2,925.00

1098	2/18/1990	Daytona Beach, FL	34	11	Pontiac	183	0	Running	$22,840.00
1099	2/25/1990	Richmond, VA	35	36	Pontiac	83	0	Crash	$2,425.00
1100	3/4/1990	Rockingham, NC	32	32	Pontiac	294	0	Engine failure	$3,775.00
1101	3/18/1990	Atlanta, GA	25	32	Pontiac	315	0	Running	$4,845.00
1102	4/1/1990	Darlington, SC	21	25	Pontiac	349	0	Engine failure	$5,390.00
1103	4/8/1990	Bristol, TN	26	28	Pontiac	328	0	Engine failure	$3,900.00
1104	4/22/1990	North Wilkesboro, NC	29	23	Pontiac	201	0	Crash	$2,475.00
1105	4/29/1990	Martinsville, VA	20	22	Pontiac	484	0	Running	$4,875.00
1106	5/6/1990	Talladega, AL	29	39	Pontiac	137	0	Running	$5,630.00
1107	5/27/1990	Charlotte, NC	27	30	Pontiac	352	0	Oil Leak	$5,650.00
1108	6/3/1990	Dover, DE	21	23	Pontiac	478	0	Running	$4,550.00
1109	6/10/1990	Sonoma, CA	26	32	Pontiac	71	0	Running	$4,420.00
1110	6/17/1990	Pocono, PA	38	22	Pontiac	94	0	Crash	$3,825.00
1111	6/24/1990	Brooklyn, MI	11	29	Pontiac	200	0	Running	$10,375.00
1112	7/7/1990	Daytona Beach, FL	36	7	Pontiac	1	0	Crash	$4,900.00
1113	7/22/1990	Pocono, PA	9	24	Pontiac	200	0	Running	$8,675.00
1114	7/29/1990	Talladega, AL	29	42	Pontiac	183	0	Running	$5,725.00
1115	8/12/1990	Watkins Glen, NY	18	28	Pontiac	89	0	Running	$5,120.00
1116	8/19/1990	Brooklyn, MI	33	22	Pontiac	128	5	Engine failure	$4,725.00
1117	8/25/1990	Bristol, TN	29	20	Pontiac	215	0	Overheating	$3,800.00
1118	9/2/1990	Darlington, SC	34	33	Pontiac	93	0	Engine failure	$1,120.00
1119	9/9/1990	Richmond, VA	21	26	Pontiac	394	0	Running	$4,075.00
1120	9/16/1990	Dover, DE	16	16	Pontiac	494	0	Running	$5,600.00
1121	9/23/1990	Martinsville, VA	29	21	Pontiac	229	0	Intake Valve	$2,250.00
1122	9/30/1990	North Wilkesboro, NC	17	28	Pontiac	397	0	Running	$4,025.00
1123	10/7/1990	Charlotte, NC	20	18	Pontiac	329	0	Running	$5,425.00
1124	10/21/1990	Rockingham, NC	21	35	Pontiac	485	0	Running	$5,350.00
1125	11/4/1990	Phoenix, AZ	23	36	Pontiac	308	0	Running	$4,300.00
1126	11/18/1990	Atlanta, GA	17	22	Pontiac	324	0	Running	$5,650.00
1127	2/19/1991	Daytona Beach, FL	19	3	Pontiac	195	0	Running	$43,120.00
1128	2/24/1991	Richmond, VA	11	23	Pontiac	398	0	Running	$7,750.00
1129	3/3/1991	Rockingham, NC	15	25	Pontiac	486	0	Running	$9,900.00
1130	3/18/1991	Atlanta, GA	38	30	Pontiac	188	0	Engine failure	$6,240.00
1131	4/7/1991	Darlington, SC	37	30	Pontiac	52	0	Engine failure	$5,750.00
1132	4/14/1991	Bristol, TN	17	33	Pontiac	496	0	Running	$7,225.00
1133	4/21/1991	North Wilkesboro, NC	16	33	Pontiac	397	0	Running	$6,550.00
1134	4/28/1991	Martinsville, VA	14	12	Pontiac	495	0	Running	$7,500.00
1135	5/6/1991	Talladega, AL	40	26	Pontiac	2	0	Crash	$5,500.00
1136	5/26/1991	Charlotte, NC	20	24	Pontiac	383	0	Crash	$10,000.00
1137	6/2/1991	Dover, DE	17	31	Pontiac	494	0	Running	$6,050.00
1138	6/9/1991	Sonoma, CA	34	39	Pontiac	59	0	Crash	$5,200.00
1139	6/16/1991	Pocono, PA	11	23	Pontiac	200	0	Running	$10,450.00
1140	6/23/1991	Brooklyn, MI	35	36	Pontiac	166	0	Valve	$7,360.00
1141	7/6/1991	Daytona Beach, FL	22	21	Pontiac	159	0	Running	$8,490.00
1142	7/21/1991	Pocono, PA	31	17	Pontiac	97	0	Crash	$6,575.00
1143	7/28/1991	Talladega, AL	18	20	Pontiac	187	0	Running	$10,880.00
1144	8/11/1991	Watkins Glen, NY	9	31	Pontiac	90	0	Running	$11,640.00
1145	8/18/1991	Brooklyn, MI	23	23	Pontiac	195	0	Running	$8,350.00
1146	8/24/1991	Bristol, TN	12	30	Pontiac	491	0	Running	$8,125.00
1147	9/1/1991	Darlington, SC	16	30	Pontiac	363	0	Running	$9,380.00
1148	9/7/1991	Richmond, VA	24	19	Pontiac	393	1	Running	$5,550.00
1149	9/15/1991	Dover, DE	20	29	Pontiac	389	0	Engine failure	$6,200.00
1150	9/22/1991	Martinsville, VA	30	29	Pontiac	348	0	Crash	$4,500.00
1151	9/29/1991	North Wilkesboro, NC	19	33	Pontiac	396	0	Running	$5,975.00
1152	10/6/1991	Charlotte, NC	12	39	Pontiac	329	0	Running	$11,400.00
1153	10/20/1991	Rockingham, NC	16	31	Pontiac	485	0	Running	$9,700.00
1154	11/3/1991	Phoenix, AZ	41	20	Pontiac	89	0	Crash	$3,250.00
1155	11/17/1991	Atlanta, GA	22	30	Pontiac	319	0	Running	$7,425.00
1156	2/16/1992	Daytona Beach, FL	16	32	Pontiac	198	0	Running	$32,530.00
1157	3/1/1992	Rockingham, NC	16	29	Pontiac	488	0	Running	$11,700.00
1158	3/8/1992	Richmond, VA	21	25	Pontiac	395	0	Running	$9,875.00
1159	3/15/1992	Atlanta, GA	16	32	Pontiac	327	0	Running	$12,470.00
1160	3/29/1992	Darlington, SC	32	30	Pontiac	161	0	Piston	$7,540.00
1161	4/5/1992	Bristol, TN	27	14	Pontiac	354	0	Running	$9,630.00
1162	4/12/1992	North Wilkesboro, NC	31	28	Pontiac	234	0	Handling	$8,610.00
1163	4/26/1992	Martinsville, VA	29	29	Pontiac	286	0	Engine failure	$7,600.00
1164	5/3/1992	Talladega, AL	15	17	Pontiac	188	0	Running	$14,660.00
1165	5/24/1992	Charlotte, NC	41	12	Pontiac	115	0	Crash	$10,600.00
1166	5/31/1992	Dover, DE	20	17	Pontiac	489	0	Running	$10,790.00
1167	6/7/1992	Sonoma, CA	21	30	Pontiac	74	0	Running	$11,055.00
1168	6/14/1992	Pocono, PA	16	21	Pontiac	198	0	Running	$11,400.00
1169	6/21/1992	Brooklyn, MI	15	14	Pontiac	198	0	Running	$14,285.00
1170	7/4/1992	Daytona Beach, FL	36	2	Pontiac	84	5	Driver fatigue	$10,925.00
1171	7/19/1992	Pocono, PA	20	7	Pontiac	199	0	Running	$11,015.00
1172	7/26/1992	Talladega, AL	15	4	Pontiac	187	0	Running	$14,325.00
1173	8/9/1992	Watkins Glen, NY	28	18	Pontiac	50	0	Running	$8,745.00
1174	8/16/1992	Brooklyn, MI	18	21	Pontiac	199	0	Running	$13,165.00
1175	8/29/1992	Bristol, TN	16	30	Pontiac	493	0	Running	$10,775.00
1176	9/6/1992	Darlington, SC	20	31	Pontiac	295	0	Running	$12,055.00
1177	9/12/1992	Richmond, VA	16	30	Pontiac	399	0	Running	$10,430.00
1178	9/20/1992	Dover, DE	28	25	Pontiac	272	0	Crash	$9,555.00
1179	9/28/1992	Martinsville, VA	18	15	Pontiac	495	0	Running	$9,355.00
1180	10/5/1992	North Wilkesboro, NC	27	21	Pontiac	390	0	Running	$7,825.00
1181	10/11/1992	Charlotte, NC	27	32	Pontiac	323	0	Running	$8,720.00
1182	10/25/1992	Rockingham, NC	25	26	Pontiac	482	0	Running	$9,850.00
1183	11/1/1992	Phoenix, AZ	22	24	Pontiac	309	0	Running	$9,510.00
1184	11/15/1992	Atlanta, GA	35	39	Pontiac	95	0	Running	$8,625.00

INDEX

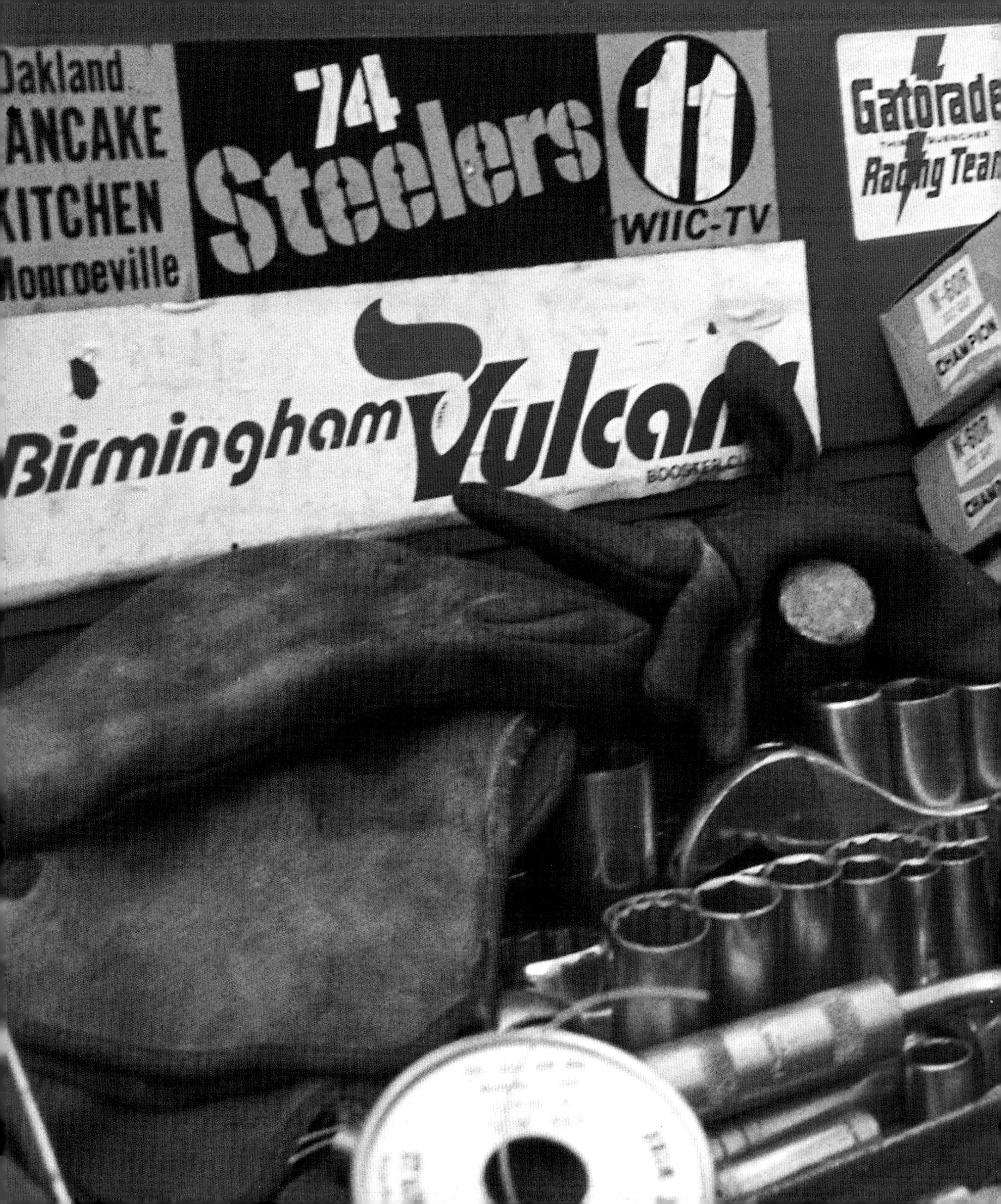
74
Steelers
11
WIIC-TV
Birmingham
Gatorade
CHAMPION